Alice in Wonderland

Alice im Wunderland

[Bilingual Edition]

English – German

by Lewis Carroll

Translated by Möwenstein

ISBN: 979-8-89513-049-0

Original text: *Alice in Wonderland* (1865) by Lewis Carroll (1832-1898)

This bilingual edition—including translation, editorial revisions, formatting, and supplementary content—is produced and edited by Mowenstein Books LLC, with the original text faithfully reproduced from public-domain sources.

While every effort has been made to ensure accuracy, minor discrepancies may occur. Readers are encouraged to consult the original text for reference.

Cover Art: Inspired by *Hustling Sunlight* by Matthew Bakkom (www.hustlingsunlight.xyz)

Möwenstein Books™ is a trademark of and imprint published by Mowenstein Books LLC.

For permissions or inquiries:

Website: mowenstein.com
Email: copyright@mowenstein.com

Mowenstein Books LLC
DE, USA

Contents

CHAPTER I. Down the Rabbit-Hole

KAPITEL I. Auf dem Weg zum Kaninchenbau

1.1 **Alice was beginning to get very tired of sitting by her sister on the bank,**
Alice war es allmählich leid,

1.2 **and of having nothing to do:**
neben ihrer Schwester auf der Bank zu sitzen und nichts zu tun zu haben:

1.3 **once or twice she had peeped into the book her sister was reading, but it had no pictures or conversations in it,**
Ein oder zwei Mal hatte sie einen Blick in das Buch geworfen, das ihre Schwester gerade las, aber es enthielt weder Bilder noch Gespräche,

1.4 **"and what is the use of a book," thought Alice,**
"und was nützt ein Buch," dachte Alice,

1.5 **"without pictures or conversations?"**
"ohne Bilder oder Gespräche?"

So she was considering in her own mind (as well as she could, for the hot day made her feel very sleepy and stupid), whether the pleasure of making a daisy-chain would be worth the trouble of getting up and picking the daisies, when suddenly a White Rabbit with pink eyes ran close by her. $\quad$ 2.1

So überlegte sie gerade (so gut sie konnte, denn der heiße Tag machte sie sehr schläfrig und dumm), ob das Vergnügen, eine Gänseblümchenkette zu machen, die Mühe des Aufstehens und des Pflückens der Gänseblümchen wert sei, als plötzlich ein weißes Kaninchen mit rosa Augen dicht an ihr vorbeilief.

There was nothing so very remarkable in that; $\quad$ 3.1

Das war nicht sonderlich bemerkenswert;

nor did Alice think it so very much out of the way to hear the Rabbit say to itself, $\quad$ 3.2

und Alice fand es auch nicht sonderlich abwegig, das Kaninchen zu sich selbst sagen zu hören,

"Oh dear! Oh dear! I shall be late!" $\quad$ 3.3

"Oh je! Oh je! Ich werde zu spät kommen!"

(when she thought it over afterwards, it occurred to her that she ought to have wondered at this, but at the time it all seemed quite natural); $\quad$ 3.4

(als sie später darüber nachdachte, fiel ihr ein, dass sie sich darüber hätte wundern sollen, aber damals schien es ganz natürlich zu sein);

3.5 but when the Rabbit actually took a watch out of its waistcoat-pocket, and looked at it, and then hurried on, Alice started to her feet, for it flashed across her mind that she had never before seen a rabbit with either a waistcoat-pocket, or a watch to take out of it, and burning with curiosity, she ran across the field after it, and fortunately was just in time to see it pop down a large rabbit-hole under the hedge.

Aber als das Kaninchen tatsächlich eine Uhr aus seiner Westentasche nahm, sie ansah und dann weiterlief, sprang Alice auf, denn ihr fiel ein, dass sie noch nie ein Kaninchen mit einer Westentasche oder einer Uhr gesehen hatte, die es aus der Tasche nehmen konnte, und vor Neugierde brennend, rannte sie über das Feld hinter ihm her und kam zum Glück gerade noch rechtzeitig, um zu sehen, wie es in einen großen Kaninchenbau unter der Hecke hinuntersprang.

4.1 In another moment down went Alice after it,

In einem anderen Moment stieg Alice hinunter und dachte nicht einmal daran,

4.2 never once considering how in the world she was to get out again.

wie sie wieder herauskommen sollte.

5.1 The rabbit-hole went straight on like a tunnel for some way, and then dipped suddenly down, so suddenly that Alice had not a moment to think about stopping herself before she found herself falling down a very deep well.

Der Kaninchenbau ging ein Stück weit geradeaus wie ein Tunnel, und dann tauchte er plötzlich ab, so plötzlich, dass Alice nicht einen Moment daran denken konnte, sich aufzuhalten, bevor sie in einen sehr tiefen Brunnen fiel.

Either the well was very deep, or she fell very slowly, for she had plenty of time as she went down to look about her and to wonder what was going to happen next.   6.1

Entweder war der Brunnen sehr tief, oder sie fiel sehr langsam, denn während sie hinunterging, hatte sie viel Zeit, sich umzusehen und sich zu fragen, was als Nächstes geschehen würde.

First, she tried to look down and make out what she was coming to, but it was too dark to see anything;   6.2

Zuerst versuchte sie, nach unten zu schauen, um zu erkennen, was auf sie zukam, aber es war zu dunkel, um irgendetwas zu sehen;

then she looked at the sides of the well,   6.3

dann schaute sie sich die Seiten des Brunnens an und bemerkte,

and noticed that they were filled with cupboards and book-shelves;   6.4

dass sie mit Schränken und Bücherregalen gefüllt waren;

here and there she saw maps and pictures hung upon pegs.   6.5

hier und da sah sie Karten und Bilder, die an Pflöcken hingen.

She took down a jar from one of the shelves as she passed; it was labelled "ORANGE MARMALADE", but to her great disappointment it was empty: 6.6

Im Vorbeigehen nahm sie ein Glas aus einem der Regale, das mit "ORANGE MARMALADE" beschriftet war, aber zu ihrer großen Enttäuschung war es leer:

6.7 she did not like to drop the jar for fear of killing somebody underneath, so managed to put it into one of the cupboards as she fell past it.

Sie wollte das Glas nicht fallen lassen, weil sie fürchtete, jemanden darunter zu töten, und so schaffte sie es, es in einen der Schränke zu stellen, als sie daran vorbeiging.

7.1 "Well!" thought Alice to herself,

"Nun," dachte Alice,

7.2 "after such a fall as this, I shall think nothing of tumbling down stairs!

"nach einem solchen Sturz werde ich nicht mehr die Treppe hinunterpurzeln!

7.3 How brave they'll all think me at home!

Für wie mutig werden mich alle zu Hause halten!

7.4 Why, I wouldn't say anything about it, even if I fell off the top of the house!"

Ich würde nichts sagen, selbst wenn ich vom Dach des Hauses fallen würde!"

7.5 (Which was very likely true.)

(Was sehr wahrscheinlich der Fall war.)

8.1 Down, down, down. Would the fall never come to an end?

Runter, runter, runter. Würde der Fall niemals enden?

8.2 "I wonder how many miles I've fallen by this time?"

"Ich frage mich, wie viele Meilen ich inzwischen gefallen bin,"

8.3 she said aloud.

sagte sie laut.

"I must be getting somewhere near the centre of the earth.　　8.4
"Ich muss mich dem Mittelpunkt der Erde nähern.

Let me see: that would be four thousand miles down, I think — "　　8.5
Mal sehen, das wären viertausend Meilen, glaube ich — "

(for, you see, Alice had learnt several things of this sort in her lessons in the schoolroom, and though this was not a very good opportunity for showing off her knowledge, as there was no one to listen to her, still it was good practice to say it over)　　8.6
(Alice hatte nämlich in der Schule einige Dinge dieser Art gelernt, und obwohl dies keine gute Gelegenheit war, ihr Wissen zu zeigen, da ihr niemand zuhörte, war es doch eine gute Übung, es zu wiederholen)

" — yes, that's about the right distance — but then I wonder what Latitude or Longitude I've got to?"　　8.7
"Ja, das ist ungefähr die richtige Entfernung, aber dann frage ich mich, auf welchem Breiten - oder Längengrad ich mich befinde?"

(Alice had no idea what Latitude was, or Longitude either, but thought they were nice grand words to say.)　　8.8
(Alice hatte keine Ahnung, was Breitengrad oder Längengrad war, aber sie fand, dass das schöne Worte waren.)

Presently she began again.　　9.1
Kurz darauf begann sie erneut.

"I wonder if I shall fall right through the earth!　　9.2
"Ich frage mich, ob ich durch die Erde fallen werde!

9.3 How funny it'll seem to come out among the people that walk with their heads downward!
Wie lustig wird es sein, unter den Leuten herauszukommen, die mit dem Kopf nach unten gehen!

9.4 The Antipathies, I think -"
Die Antipathen, denke ich -"

9.5 (she was rather glad there was no one listening, this time, as it didn't sound at all the right word)
(sie war froh, dass diesmal niemand zuhörte, denn es klang überhaupt nicht nach dem richtigen Wort) -

9.6 "- but I shall have to ask them what the name of the country is, you know.
"aber ich muss sie fragen, wie das Land heißt, wissen Sie.

9.7 Please, Ma'am, is this New Zealand or Australia?"
Bitte, Ma'am, ist das Neuseeland oder Australien?"

9.8 (and she tried to curtsey as she spoke -
(und sie versuchte, einen Knicks zu machen, während sie sprach -

9.9 fancy curtseying as you're falling through the air!
ein schöner Knicks, wenn man durch die Luft fällt!

9.10 Do you think you could manage it?)
Glaubst du, du könntest es schaffen?)

9.11 "And what an ignorant little girl she'll think me for asking!
"Und für was für ein dummes kleines Mädchen wird sie mich halten, wenn ich das frage!

No, it'll never do to ask: perhaps I shall see it written up somewhere." 9.12

Nein, fragen geht nicht, vielleicht steht es ja irgendwo geschrieben."

Down, down, down. There was nothing else to do, 10.1

Runter, runter, runter. Es gab nichts anderes zu tun,

so Alice soon began talking again. 10.2

und so begann Alice bald wieder zu sprechen.

"Dinah'll miss me very much to-night, I should think!" 10.3

"Dinah wird mich heute Abend sehr vermissen, denke ich!"

(Dinah was the cat.) 10.4

(Dinah war die Katze.)

"I hope they'll remember her saucer of milk at tea-time. 10.5

"Ich hoffe, sie werden an ihre Milchschüssel zur Teestunde denken.

Dinah my dear! I wish you were down here with me! 10.6

Dinah, meine Liebe! Ich wünschte, du wärst hier unten bei mir!

There are no mice in the air, I'm afraid, but you might catch a bat, and that's very like a mouse, you know. 10.7

Ich fürchte, es gibt keine Mäuse in der Luft, aber du könntest eine Fledermaus fangen, und die ist einer Maus sehr ähnlich, weißt du.

But do cats eat bats, I wonder?" 10.8

Aber ob Katzen Fledermäuse fressen, frage ich mich?"

10.9 And here Alice began to get rather sleepy, and went on saying to herself, in a dreamy sort of way:
Und hier wurde Alice ziemlich schläfrig und sagte immer wieder verträumt zu sich selbst:

10.10 "Do cats eat bats? Do cats eat bats?"
"Fressen Katzen Fledermäuse? Fressen Katzen Fledermäuse?"

10.11 and sometimes, "Do bats eat cats?"
und manchmal: "Fressen Fledermäuse Katzen?"

10.12 for, you see, as she couldn't answer either question, it didn't much matter which way she put it.
denn da sie keine der beiden Fragen beantworten konnte, war es egal, wie sie sie stellte.

10.13 She felt that she was dozing off, and had just begun to dream that she was walking hand in hand with Dinah, and saying to her very earnestly:
Sie hatte das Gefühl, einzuschlafen, und träumte gerade, dass sie Hand in Hand mit Dinah spazieren ging und zu ihr ganz ernsthaft sagte:

10.14 "Now, Dinah, tell me the truth:
"Nun, Dinah, sag mir die Wahrheit:

10.15 did you ever eat a bat?"
Hast du jemals eine Fledermaus gegessen?"

10.16 when suddenly, thump! thump! down she came upon a heap of sticks and dry leaves, and the fall was over.
als sie plötzlich, dumpf, dumpf, auf einen Haufen von Stöcken und trockenen Blättern fiel und der Sturz vorbei war.

Alice was not a bit hurt, and she jumped up on to her feet in a moment:

11.1

Alice war kein bisschen verletzt und sprang sofort auf:

she looked up, but it was all dark overhead;

11.2

Sie schaute nach oben, aber über ihr war alles dunkel;

before her was another long passage, and the White Rabbit was still in sight, hurrying down it.

11.3

vor ihr lag ein weiterer langer Gang, und das Weiße Kaninchen war immer noch in Sicht und eilte ihn hinunter.

There was not a moment to be lost: away went Alice like the wind, and was just in time to hear it say, as it turned a corner:

11.4

Es galt, keine Zeit zu verlieren: Alice lief los wie der Wind und kam gerade noch rechtzeitig, um zu hören, wie es um eine Ecke bog und sagte:

"Oh my ears and whiskers, how late it's getting!"

11.5

"Oh je, meine Ohren und Schnurrhaare, wie spät es schon ist!"

She was close behind it when she turned the corner, but the Rabbit was no longer to be seen:

11.6

Sie war dicht hinter ihm, als es um die Ecke bog, aber das Kaninchen war nicht mehr zu sehen:

she found herself in a long, low hall, which was lit up by a row of lamps hanging from the roof.

11.7

Sie fand sich in einer langen, niedrigen Halle wieder, die von einer Reihe von Lampen, die von der Decke hingen, beleuchtet wurde.

12.1 There were doors all round the hall, but they were all locked; and when Alice had been all the way down one side and up the other, trying every door, she walked sadly down the middle, wondering how she was ever to get out again.

Überall in der Halle gab es Türen, aber sie waren alle verschlossen, und als Alice den ganzen Weg von einer Seite zur anderen gegangen war und jede Tür ausprobiert hatte, ging sie traurig durch die Mitte und fragte sich, wie sie jemals wieder herauskommen sollte.

13.1 Suddenly she came upon a little three-legged table, all made of solid glass; there was nothing on it except a tiny golden key, and Alice's first thought was that it might belong to one of the doors of the hall; but, alas!

Plötzlich stieß sie auf einen kleinen dreibeinigen Tisch, ganz aus massivem Glas, auf dem nichts lag außer einem winzigen goldenen Schlüssel, und Alices erster Gedanke war, dass er zu einer der Türen des Saales gehören könnte; aber ach!

13.2 either the locks were too large, or the key was too small, but at any rate it would not open any of them.

entweder waren die Schlösser zu groß oder der Schlüssel zu klein, jedenfalls ließ sich damit keine der Türen öffnen.

13.3 However, on the second time round, she came upon a low curtain she had not noticed before, and behind it was a little door about fifteen inches high:

Doch beim zweiten Mal stieß sie auf einen niedrigen Vorhang, den sie vorher nicht bemerkt hatte, und dahinter befand sich eine kleine Tür, die etwa fünfzehn Zentimeter hoch war:

13.4 she tried the little golden key in the lock,

Sie probierte den kleinen goldenen Schlüssel im Schloss aus,

11

and to her great delight it fitted!   13.5
und zu ihrer großen Freude passte er!

Alice opened the door and found that it led into a   14.1
small passage, not much larger than a rat-hole:
Alice öffnete die Tür und stellte fest, dass sie in einen
kleinen Gang führte, der nicht viel größer war als ein
Rattenloch:

she knelt down and looked along the passage into the   14.2
loveliest garden you ever saw.
Sie kniete nieder und blickte den Gang entlang in den
schönsten Garten, den man je gesehen hatte.

How she longed to get out of that dark hall, and   14.3
wander about among those beds of bright flowers
and those cool fountains, but she could not even get
her head through the doorway;
Wie sehr sehnte sie sich danach, aus dieser dunklen
Halle herauszukommen und zwischen den Beeten mit
den leuchtenden Blumen und den kühlen Brunnen
umherzuwandern, aber sie konnte nicht einmal ihren
Kopf durch die Türöffnung stecken;

"and even if my head would go through,"   14.4
"und selbst wenn mein Kopf hindurchginge,"

thought poor Alice,   14.5
dachte die arme Alice,

"it would be of very little use without my shoulders.   14.6
"wäre er ohne meine Schultern von sehr geringem Nutzen.

Oh, how I wish I could shut up like a telescope!   14.7
Oh, ich wünschte, ich könnte mich wie ein Teleskop
schließen!

14.8 I think I could, if I only knew how to begin."

Ich glaube, ich könnte es, wenn ich nur wüsste, wie ich anfangen soll."

14.9 For, you see, so many out-of-the-way things had happened lately, that Alice had begun to think that very few things indeed were really impossible.

Denn in letzter Zeit waren so viele ungewöhnliche Dinge passiert, dass Alice angefangen hatte zu glauben, dass nur sehr wenige Dinge wirklich unmöglich waren.

15.1 There seemed to be no use in waiting by the little door, so she went back to the table, half hoping she might find another key on it, or at any rate a book of rules for shutting people up like telescopes:

Es schien keinen Sinn zu haben, an der kleinen Tür zu warten, und so ging sie zurück zum Tisch, halb in der Hoffnung, einen anderen Schlüssel darauf zu finden, oder zumindest ein Buch mit Regeln, wie man Leute wie Teleskope einsperrt:

15.2 this time she found a little bottle on it, ("which certainly was not here before,"

diesmal fand sie eine kleine Flasche darauf, ("die vorhin sicher nicht hier war,"

15.3 said Alice,) and round the neck of the bottle was a paper label, with the words

sagte Alice), und um den Hals der Flasche war ein Papieretikett mit den Worten

15.4 "DRINK ME," beautifully printed on it in large letters.

"DRINK ME," schön in großen Buchstaben darauf gedruckt.

It was all very well to say "Drink me,"   16.1

Es war schön und gut, "Trink mich"

but the wise little Alice was not going to do that in a   16.2
hurry.

zu sagen, aber die kluge kleine Alice hatte nicht vor, das in
aller Eile zu tun.

"No, I'll look first," she said,   16.3

"Nein, ich werde erst einmal nachsehen," sagte sie,

"and see whether it's marked 'poison' or not";   16.4

"ob da 'Gift' draufsteht oder nicht";

for she had read several nice little histories about   16.5
children who had got burnt, and eaten up by wild
beasts and other unpleasant things, all because they
would not remember the simple rules their friends
had taught them:

denn sie hatte schon einige nette kleine Geschichten über
Kinder gelesen, die sich verbrannt, von wilden Tieren
aufgefressen und andere unangenehme Dinge erlebt hatten,
nur weil sie sich nicht an die einfachen Regeln erinnern
wollten, die ihre Freunde ihnen beigebracht hatten:

such as, that a red-hot poker will burn you if you   16.6
hold it too long; and that if you cut your finger very
deeply with a knife, it usually bleeds; and she had
never forgotten that, if you drink much from a bottle
marked

Dass man sich an einem glühenden Schürhaken verbrennt,
wenn man ihn zu lange in der Hand hält, dass man sich mit
einem Messer sehr tief in den Finger schneidet und dass es
gewöhnlich blutet, und dass man, wenn man viel aus einer
Flasche trinkt, die mit

"poison,"   16.7

"Gift"

16.8   it is almost certain to disagree with you, sooner or later.

beschriftet ist, fast sicher ist, dass sie einem früher oder später nicht mehr schmeckt, hatte sie nie vergessen.

17.1   However, this bottle was not marked "poison,"

Diese Flasche war jedoch nicht mit "Gift"

17.2   so Alice ventured to taste it, and finding it very nice, (it had, in fact, a sort of mixed flavour of cherry-tart, custard, pine-apple, roast turkey, toffee, and hot buttered toast,) she very soon finished it off.

gekennzeichnet, so dass Alice es wagte, sie zu probieren, und da sie sie sehr gut fand (sie hatte in der Tat eine Art gemischten Geschmack von Kirschtorte, Vanillepudding, Ananas, gebratenem Truthahn, Toffee und heißem gebutterten Toast), trank sie sie sehr bald aus.

19.1   "What a curious feeling!" said Alice;

"Was für ein merkwürdiges Gefühl!" sagte Alice;

19.2   "I must be shutting up like a telescope."

"ich muss wie ein Teleskop geschlossen sein."

20.1   And so it was indeed:

Und so war es auch:

she was now only ten inches high, and her face brightened up at the thought that she was now the right size for going through the little door into that lovely garden.

20.2

Sie war jetzt nur noch zehn Zentimeter groß, und ihr Gesicht erhellte sich bei dem Gedanken, dass sie nun die richtige Größe hatte, um durch die kleine Tür in diesen schönen Garten zu gehen.

First, however, she waited for a few minutes to see if she was going to shrink any further:

20.3

Doch zunächst wartete sie ein paar Minuten, um zu sehen, ob sie noch weiter schrumpfen würde:

she felt a little nervous about this;

20.4

Sie fühlte sich dabei ein wenig nervös,

"for it might end, you know," said Alice to herself,

20.5

"denn es könnte damit enden," sagte Alice zu sich selbst,

"in my going out altogether, like a candle.

20.6

"dass ich ganz erlösche, wie eine Kerze.

I wonder what I should be like then?"

20.7

Ich frage mich, wie ich dann wohl aussehen würde?"

And she tried to fancy what the flame of a candle is like after the candle is blown out, for she could not remember ever having seen such a thing.

20.8

Und sie versuchte sich vorzustellen, wie die Flamme einer Kerze aussieht, nachdem sie ausgeblasen wurde, denn sie konnte sich nicht erinnern, so etwas jemals gesehen zu haben.

21.1 **After a while, finding that nothing more happened, she decided on going into the garden at once;**
Als sie nach einer Weile feststellte, dass nichts weiter geschah, beschloss sie, sofort in den Garten zu gehen;

21.2 **but, alas for poor Alice!**
aber, ach, die arme Alice!

21.3 **when she got to the door, she found she had forgotten the little golden key, and when she went back to the table for it, she found she could not possibly reach it:**
als sie zur Tür kam, stellte sie fest, dass sie den kleinen goldenen Schlüssel vergessen hatte, und als sie zurück zum Tisch ging, um ihn zu holen, stellte sie fest, dass sie ihn unmöglich erreichen konnte:

21.4 **she could see it quite plainly through the glass, and she tried her best to climb up one of the legs of the table, but it was too slippery;**
sie konnte ihn ganz deutlich durch das Glas sehen, und sie versuchte ihr Bestes, um an einem der Tischbeine hinaufzuklettern, aber es war zu rutschig;

21.5 **and when she had tired herself out with trying,**
und als sie sich mit ihren Versuchen erschöpft hatte,

21.6 **the poor little thing sat down and cried.**
setzte sich das arme kleine Ding hin und weinte.

22.1 **"Come, there's no use in crying like that!"**
"Komm, es hat keinen Sinn, so zu weinen,"

22.2 **said Alice to herself, rather sharply;**
sagte Alice zu sich selbst, ziemlich scharf;

22.3 **"I advise you to leave off this minute!"**
"ich rate dir, es jetzt zu lassen!"

She generally gave herself very good advice, (though she very seldom followed it), and sometimes she scolded herself so severely as to bring tears into her eyes; 22.4

Im Allgemeinen gab sie sich selbst sehr gute Ratschläge (obwohl sie sie nur selten befolgte), und manchmal schimpfte sie so heftig mit sich selbst, dass ihr die Tränen in die Augen stiegen;

and once she remembered trying to box her own ears for having cheated herself in a game of croquet she was playing against herself, for this curious child was very fond of pretending to be two people. 22.5

und einmal erinnerte sie sich daran, wie sie versuchte, sich selbst eine Ohrfeige zu verpassen, weil sie sich bei einem Krocketspiel, das sie gegen sich selbst spielte, betrogen hatte, denn dieses neugierige Kind liebte es sehr, sich für zwei Personen auszugeben.

"But it's no use now," thought poor Alice, 22.6

"Aber es hat keinen Sinn mehr," dachte die arme Alice,

"to pretend to be two people! 22.7

"so zu tun, als ob man zwei Personen wäre!

Why, 22.8

Es ist ja kaum noch genug von mir übrig,

there's hardly enough of me left to make one respectable person!" 22.9

um eine anständige Person zu sein!"

23.1 Soon her eye fell on a little glass box that was lying under the table: she opened it, and found in it a very small cake, on which the words

Bald fiel ihr Blick auf eine kleine Glasschachtel, die unter dem Tisch lag; sie öffnete sie und fand darin einen sehr kleinen Kuchen, auf dem mit Johannisbeeren schön die Worte

23.2 "EAT ME" were beautifully marked in currants.

"EAT ME" geschrieben standen.

23.3 "Well, I'll eat it," said Alice,

"Nun, ich werde ihn essen," sagte Alice,

23.4 "and if it makes me grow larger,

"und wenn ich dadurch größer werde,

23.5 I can reach the key;

kann ich den Schlüssel erreichen;

23.6 and if it makes me grow smaller,

und wenn ich dadurch kleiner werde,

23.7 I can creep under the door;

kann ich unter der Tür durchkriechen;

23.8 so either way I'll get into the garden, and I don't care which happens!"

so oder so werde ich in den Garten gelangen, und es ist mir egal, was passiert!"

24.1 She ate a little bit, and said anxiously to herself,

Sie aß ein wenig davon und fragte sich ängstlich:

"Which way? Which way?", holding her hand on the 24.2
top of her head to feel which way it was growing, and
she was quite surprised to find that she remained the
same size:

"Wohin? Sie hielt ihre Hand auf ihren Kopf, um zu fühlen,
in welche Richtung er wuchs, und war ziemlich überrascht,
als sie feststellte, dass er die gleiche Größe behielt:

to be sure, this generally happens when one eats cake, 24.3
but Alice had got so much into the way of expecting
nothing but out-of-the-way things to happen, that it
seemed quite dull and stupid for life to go on in the
common way.

Das passiert zwar im Allgemeinen, wenn man Kuchen
isst, aber Alice hatte sich so sehr daran gewöhnt, dass sie
nur noch außergewöhnliche Dinge erwartete, dass es ihr
ziemlich langweilig und dumm vorkam, wenn das Leben
auf die übliche Weise weiterging.

So she set to work, and very soon finished off the 25.1
cake.

Also machte sie sich an die Arbeit und war schon bald mit
dem Kuchen fertig.

CHAPTER II. The Pool of Tears

KAPITEL II. Der Teich der Tränen

1.1 "Curiouser and curiouser!"
"Seltsamer und seltsamer!"

1.2 cried Alice (she was so much surprised, that for the moment she quite forgot how to speak good English);
rief Alice (sie war so überrascht, dass sie für einen Moment ganz vergessen hatte, wie man gut Englisch spricht);

1.3 "now I'm opening out like the largest telescope that ever was!
"jetzt öffne ich mich wie das größte Teleskop, das es je gab!

1.4 Good-bye, feet!"
Auf Wiedersehen, Füße!"

1.5 (for when she looked down at her feet, they seemed to be almost out of sight, they were getting so far off).
(denn als sie auf ihre Füße hinunterblickte, schienen sie fast außer Sichtweite zu sein, so weit waren sie weg).

"Oh, my poor little feet, I wonder who will put on your shoes and stockings for you now, dears? 1.6
"Oh, meine armen kleinen Füße, ich frage mich, wer euch jetzt die Schuhe und Strümpfe anziehen wird, meine Lieben?

I'm sure I shan't be able! 1.7
Ich bin sicher, dass ich es nicht kann!

I shall be a great deal too far off to trouble myself about you: 1.8
Ich werde viel zu weit weg sein, um mich um euch zu kümmern:

you must manage the best way you can; 1.9
ihr müsst es so gut wie möglich machen;

— but I must be kind to them," thought Alice, 1.10
aber ich muss nett zu ihnen sein," dachte Alice,

"or perhaps they won't walk the way I want to go! 1.11
"sonst gehen sie vielleicht nicht den Weg, den ich gehen will!

Let me see: 1.12
Lass mich mal sehen:

I'll give them a new pair of boots every Christmas." 1.13
Ich werde ihnen jedes Jahr zu Weihnachten ein neues Paar Stiefel schenken."

And she went on planning to herself how she would manage it. 2.1
Und sie überlegte sich, wie sie es anstellen würde.

"They must go by the carrier," she thought; 2.2
"Sie müssen mit dem Boten gehen," dachte sie,

2.3   "and how funny it'll seem,
"und wie komisch wird es aussehen,

2.4   sending presents to one's own feet!
wenn man die Geschenke zu seinen eigenen Füßen schickt!

2.5   And how odd the directions will look!
Und wie seltsam wird die Wegbeschreibung aussehen!

3.1   Alice's Right Foot, Esq.,
Alice's Right Foot, Esq.,

3.2   Hearthrug, near the Fender, (with Alice's love).
Hearthrug, nahe dem Fender, (mit Alices Liebe).

4.1   Oh dear, what nonsense I'm talking!"
Oh je, was rede ich da für einen Unsinn!"

5.1   Just then her head struck against the roof of the hall:
in fact she was now more than nine feet high, and she
at once took up the little golden key and hurried off to
the garden door.
In diesem Augenblick stieß sie mit dem Kopf gegen das
Dach des Saales, denn sie war nun mehr als neun Fuß
hoch, nahm den kleinen goldenen Schlüssel und eilte zur
Gartentür.

6.1   Poor Alice!
Die arme Alice!

6.2   It was as much as she could do, lying down on one
side, to look through into the garden with one eye;
but to get through was more hopeless than ever:
Sie legte sich auf die Seite und versuchte, mit einem Auge
in den Garten zu schauen, aber es war hoffnungsloser als je
zuvor:

she sat down and began to cry again.   6.3

Sie setzte sich hin und begann wieder zu weinen.

"You ought to be ashamed of yourself," said Alice,   7.1

"Du solltest dich schämen," sagte Alice,

"a great girl like you," (she might well say this),   7.2

"ein großartiges Mädchen wie du," (das konnte sie wohl
sagen),

"to go on crying in this way! Stop this moment,   7.3

"auf diese Weise zu weinen! Hör sofort auf,

I tell you!"   7.4

sage ich dir!"

But she went on all the same, shedding gallons of   7.5
tears, until there was a large pool all round her, about
four inches deep and reaching half down the hall.

Aber sie weinte trotzdem weiter und vergoss literweise
Tränen, bis um sie herum eine große Lache entstand,
die etwa vier Zentimeter tief war und den halben Flur
hinunterreichte.

After a time she heard a little pattering of feet in the   8.1
distance, and she hastily dried her eyes to see what
was coming.

Nach einer Weile hörte sie in der Ferne ein leises
Fußgetrappel, und sie trocknete eilig die Augen, um zu
sehen, was da kam.

8.2 It was the White Rabbit returning, splendidly dressed, with a pair of white kid gloves in one hand and a large fan in the other: he came trotting along in a great hurry, muttering to himself as he came:

Es war das Weiße Kaninchen, das zurückkehrte, prächtig gekleidet, mit einem Paar weißer Ziegenhandschuhe in der einen und einem großen Fächer in der anderen Hand: es kam in großer Eile dahergetrabt und murmelte vor sich hin:

8.3 "Oh! the Duchess, the Duchess! Oh!

"Oh! die Herzogin, die Herzogin! Oh!

8.4 won't she be savage if I've kept her waiting!"

wird sie nicht wütend sein, wenn ich sie warten lasse!"

8.5 Alice felt so desperate that she was ready to ask help of any one;

Alice fühlte sich so verzweifelt, dass sie bereit war, jeden um Hilfe zu bitten;

8.6 so, when the Rabbit came near her, she began, in a low, timid voice:

als das Kaninchen in ihre Nähe kam, begann sie mit leiser, ängstlicher Stimme:

8.7 "If you please, sir — "

"Wenn Sie bitte, mein Herr — "

8.8 The Rabbit started violently, dropped the white kid gloves and the fan, and skurried away into the darkness as hard as he could go.

Das Kaninchen schreckte auf, ließ die weißen Samthandschuhe und den Fächer fallen und huschte so schnell er konnte in die Dunkelheit davon.

Alice took up the fan and gloves, and, as the hall was very hot, she kept fanning herself all the time she went on talking: 9.1

Alice nahm den Fächer und die Handschuhe zur Hand, und da es im Saal sehr heiß war, fächelte sie sich immer wieder Luft zu, während sie weitersprach:

"Dear, dear! How queer everything is to-day! 9.2

"Oje, oje! Wie seltsam heute alles ist!

And yesterday things went on just as usual. 9.3

Und gestern ging alles so weiter wie immer.

I wonder if I've been changed in the night? 9.4

Ich frage mich, ob ich in der Nacht verwandelt worden bin?

Let me think: 9.5

Lass mich nachdenken:

was I the same when I got up this morning? 9.6

War ich dieselbe, als ich heute Morgen aufstand?

I almost think I can remember feeling a little different. 9.7

Ich glaube fast, ich erinnere mich, dass ich mich ein wenig anders gefühlt habe.

But if I'm not the same, the next question is, Who in the world am I? 9.8

Aber wenn ich nicht derselbe bin, lautet die nächste Frage: Wer in aller Welt bin ich?

Ah, that's the great puzzle!" 9.9

Ah, das ist das große Rätsel!"

9.10 And she began thinking over all the children she knew that were of the same age as herself, to see if she could have been changed for any of them.

Und sie begann, über alle Kinder nachzudenken, die sie kannte und die im gleichen Alter wie sie selbst waren, um zu sehen, ob sie für eines von ihnen verändert worden sein könnte.

10.1 "I'm sure I'm not Ada," she said,

"Ich bin sicher, daß ich nicht Ada bin," sagte sie,

10.2 "for her hair goes in such long ringlets,

"denn ihr Haar hat so lange Locken,

10.3 and mine doesn't go in ringlets at all;

und meines hat überhaupt keine Locken;

10.4 and I'm sure I can't be Mabel, for I know all sorts of things, and she, oh!

und ich bin sicher, daß ich nicht Mabel sein kann, denn ich weiß alles Mögliche, und sie, oh!

10.5 she knows such a very little!

sie weiß so wenig!

10.6 Besides, she's she, and I'm I, and - oh dear,

Außerdem ist sie sie, und ich bin ich, und - oh je,

10.7 how puzzling it all is!

wie rätselhaft das alles ist!

10.8 I'll try if I know all the things I used to know.

Ich will es versuchen, wenn ich all die Dinge weiß, die ich früher wusste.

10.9 Let me see:

Mal sehen:

four times five is twelve, and four times six is
thirteen, and four times seven is -

10.10

vier mal fünf ist zwölf, und vier mal sechs ist dreizehn, und
vier mal sieben ist -

oh dear! I shall never get to twenty at that rate!

10.11

oh je! Bei dem Tempo komme ich nie bis zwanzig!

However, the Multiplication Table doesn't signify:

10.12

Aber die Multiplikationstabelle ist nicht aussagekräftig:

let's try Geography.

10.13

Versuchen wir es mit Geographie.

London is the capital of Paris, and Paris is the capital
of Rome, and Rome — no, that's all wrong, I'm
certain!

10.14

London ist die Hauptstadt von Paris, und Paris ist die
Hauptstadt von Rom, und Rom — nein, das ist alles falsch,
da bin ich mir sicher!

I must have been changed for Mabel!

10.15

Ich muss mit Mabel verwechselt worden sein!

I'll try and say 'How doth the little — "'

10.16

Ich werde versuchen, zu sagen, 'Wie geht es dem
kleinen — "'

and she crossed her hands on her lap as if she were
saying lessons, and began to repeat it, but her voice
sounded hoarse and strange, and the words did not
come the same as they used to do: —

10.17

und sie kreuzte die Hände auf ihrem Schoß, als ob sie
Unterricht geben würde, und begann es zu wiederholen,
aber ihre Stimme klang heiser und seltsam, und die Worte
kamen nicht so, wie sie es sonst taten: —

"How doth the little crocodile	"Wie geht es dem kleinen Krokodil
Improve his shining tail,	Verbessern Sie seinen glänzenden Schwanz,
And pour the waters of the Nile	Und gieße das Wasser des Nils
On every golden scale!	Auf jeder Goldwaage!
"How cheerfully he seems to grin,	"Wie fröhlich er zu grinsen scheint,
How neatly spread his claws,	Wie fein säuberlich er seine Krallen ausbreitet,
And welcome little fishes in	Und begrüßen kleine Fische in
With gently smiling jaws!"	Mit sanft lächelnden Kiefern!"

12.1 "I'm sure those are not the right words,"
"Ich bin sicher, dass das nicht die richtigen Worte sind,"

12.2 said poor Alice, and her eyes filled with tears again as she went on,
sagte die arme Alice, und ihre Augen füllten sich wieder mit Tränen, als sie fortfuhr:

12.3 "I must be Mabel after all, and I shall have to go and live in that poky little house, and have next to no toys to play with, and oh!
"Ich muss also doch Mabel sein, und ich werde in diesem schäbigen kleinen Haus leben müssen und so gut wie kein Spielzeug haben, mit dem ich spielen kann, und ach!

ever so many lessons to learn! No,
so viele Lektionen lernen müssen! Nein,

12.4

I've made up my mind about it; if I'm Mabel,
ich habe mich entschieden; wenn ich Mabel bin,

12.5

I'll stay down here!
bleibe ich hier unten!

12.6

It'll be no use their putting their heads down and saying:
Es hat keinen Zweck, dass sie den Kopf senken und sagen:

12.7

'Come up again, dear!'
"Komm wieder hoch, Liebes!'

12.8

I shall only look up and say 'Who am I then?
Ich werde nur aufschauen und sagen: 'Wer bin ich denn?

12.9

Tell me that first, and then, if I like being that person, I'll come up: if not, I'll stay down here till I'm somebody else' -
Sagen Sie mir das zuerst, und dann, wenn es mir gefällt, diese Person zu sein, komme ich hoch; wenn nicht, bleibe ich hier unten, bis ich jemand anderes bin -

12.10

but, oh dear!" cried Alice, with a sudden burst of tears,
aber, oh je!" rief Alice mit einem plötzlichen Tränenausbruch,

12.11

"I do wish they would put their heads down!
"ich wünschte, sie würden ihre Köpfe senken!

12.12

I am so very tired of being all alone here!"
Ich habe es so sehr satt, hier ganz allein zu sein!"

12.13

13.1 As she said this she looked down at her hands, and was surprised to see that she had put on one of the Rabbit's little white kid gloves while she was talking.

Als sie dies sagte, schaute sie auf ihre Hände hinunter und stellte überrascht fest, dass sie einen der kleinen weißen Ziegenhandschuhe des Kaninchens angezogen hatte, während sie sprach.

13.2 "How can I have done that?" she thought.

"Wie konnte ich das nur tun?" dachte sie.

13.3 "I must be growing small again."

"Ich muss wohl wieder klein geworden sein."

13.4 She got up and went to the table to measure herself by it, and found that, as nearly as she could guess, she was now about two feet high, and was going on shrinking rapidly:

Sie stand auf und ging zum Tisch, um sich daran zu messen, und stellte fest, dass sie, soweit sie es einschätzen konnte, jetzt etwa einen Meter groß war und immer weiter schrumpfte:

13.5 she soon found out that the cause of this was the fan she was holding, and she dropped it hastily, just in time to avoid shrinking away altogether.

Sie fand bald heraus, dass die Ursache dafür der Fächer war, den sie in der Hand hielt, und sie ließ ihn eilig fallen, gerade noch rechtzeitig, um nicht ganz zu schrumpfen.

14.1 "That was a narrow escape!"

"Das war ein knappes Entrinnen,"

14.2 said Alice, a good deal frightened at the sudden change, but very glad to find herself still in existence;

sagte Alice, sehr erschrocken über die plötzliche Verwandlung, aber sehr froh, daß sie noch lebte;

"and now for the garden!" 14.3
"und jetzt in den Garten!"

and she ran with all speed back to the little door: but, 14.4
alas!
und sie lief mit aller Eile zum Türchen zurück: aber ach!

the little door was shut again, and the little golden 14.5
key was lying on the glass table as before,
das Türchen war wieder geschlossen, und der kleine
goldene Schlüssel lag wie zuvor auf dem Glastisch,

"and things are worse than ever," thought the poor 14.6
child,
"und es ist schlimmer denn je," dachte das arme Kind,

"for I never was so small as this before, never! 14.7
"denn so klein war ich noch nie, nie!

And I declare it's too bad, that it is!" 14.8
Und ich sage, es ist zu schlimm, das ist es!"

As she said these words her foot slipped, and in 15.1
another moment, splash!
Während sie diese Worte sagte, rutschte sie mit dem Fuß
aus, und im nächsten Moment, platsch!

she was up to her chin in salt water. 15.2
stand sie bis zum Kinn im Salzwasser.

Her first idea was that she had somehow fallen into 15.3
the sea,
Ihr erster Gedanke war, dass sie irgendwie ins Meer
gefallen war,

"and in that case I can go back by railway," 15.4
"dann kann ich ja mit der Eisenbahn zurückfahren,"

15.5 she said to herself.

sagte sie zu sich selbst.

15.6 (Alice had been to the seaside once in her life, and had come to the general conclusion, that wherever you go to on the English coast you find a number of bathing machines in the sea, some children digging in the sand with wooden spades, then a row of lodging houses, and behind them a railway station.)

(Alice war einmal in ihrem Leben am Meer gewesen und war zu dem Schluss gekommen, dass man überall an der englischen Küste eine Reihe von Bademaschinen im Meer findet, einige Kinder, die mit Holzspaten im Sand graben, dann eine Reihe von Unterkünften und dahinter einen Bahnhof.)

15.7 However, she soon made out that she was in the pool of tears which she had wept when she was nine feet high.

Sie stellte jedoch bald fest, dass sie sich in dem Tränenbad befand, das sie geweint hatte, als sie neun Fuß groß war.

16.1 "I wish I hadn't cried so much!"

"Ich wünschte, ich hätte nicht so viel geweint,"

16.2 said Alice, as she swam about, trying to find her way out.

sagte Alice, während sie herumschwamm und versuchte, einen Ausweg zu finden.

16.3 "I shall be punished for it now, I suppose, by being drowned in my own tears!

"Jetzt werde ich wohl dafür bestraft werden, indem ich in meinen eigenen Tränen ertrinke!

16.4 That will be a queer thing, to be sure!

Das wird sicher eine seltsame Sache sein!

However, everything is queer to- day." 16.5

Aber heute ist alles seltsam."

Just then she heard something splashing about in the 17.1
pool a little way off, and she swam nearer to make out
what it was:

In diesem Moment hörte sie etwas im Becken plätschern,
und sie schwamm näher heran, um zu sehen, was es war:

at first she thought it must be a walrus or 17.2
hippopotamus, but then she remembered how small
she was now, and she soon made out that it was only a
mouse that had slipped in like herself.

zuerst dachte sie, es müsse ein Walross oder ein Nilpferd
sein, aber dann erinnerte sie sich daran, wie klein sie jetzt
war, und sie erkannte bald, dass es nur eine Maus war, die
wie sie hineingeschlüpft war.

"Would it be of any use, now," thought Alice, 18.1

"Würde es etwas nützen," dachte Alice,

"to speak to this mouse? 18.2

"mit dieser Maus zu sprechen?

Everything is so out-of-the-way down here, that 18.3
I should think very likely it can talk: at any rate,
there's no harm in trying."

Hier unten ist alles so abgelegen, dass ich denke, dass sie
sehr wohl sprechen kann; jedenfalls kann es nicht schaden,
es zu versuchen."

So she began: 18.4

Also begann sie:

"O Mouse, do you know the way out of this pool? 18.5

"O Maus, weißt du, wie man aus diesem Teich
herauskommt?

34

18.6 I am very tired of swimming about here, O Mouse!"

Ich bin es sehr leid, hier herumzuschwimmen, Maus!"

18.7 (Alice thought this must be the right way of speaking to a mouse: she had never done such a thing before, but she remembered having seen in her brother's Latin Grammar,

(Alice dachte, das müsse die richtige Art sein, mit einer Maus zu sprechen: sie hatte so etwas noch nie getan, aber sie erinnerte sich, in der lateinischen Grammatik ihres Bruders gesehen zu haben:

18.8 "A mouse — of a mouse — to a mouse — a mouse — O mouse!

"Eine Maus von einer Maus zu einer Maus - eine Maus - eine Maus"!)

18.9 ") The Mouse looked at her rather inquisitively, and seemed to her to wink with one of its little eyes, but it said nothing.

Die Maus schaute sie neugierig an und schien ihr mit einem ihrer kleinen Augen zuzuzwinkern, aber sie sagte nichts.

19.1 "Perhaps it doesn't understand English," thought Alice;

"Vielleicht versteht sie kein Englisch," dachte Alice,

19.2 "I daresay it's a French mouse, come over with William the Conqueror."

"ich wage zu behaupten, dass es eine französische Maus ist, die mit Wilhelm dem Eroberer gekommen ist."

(For, with all her knowledge of history, Alice had no very clear notion how long ago anything had happened.) 19.3

(Denn trotz all ihrer Geschichtskenntnisse hatte Alice keine klare Vorstellung davon, wie lange es her war, dass irgendetwas passiert war.)

So she began again: "Où est ma chatte?" 19.4

Also fing sie wieder an: "Où est ma chatte?"

which was the first sentence in her French lesson-book. 19.5

das war der erste Satz in ihrem Französisch-Lehrbuch.

The Mouse gave a sudden leap out of the water, and seemed to quiver all over with fright. 19.6

Die Maus machte einen plötzlichen Sprung aus dem Wasser und schien vor Schreck am ganzen Körper zu zittern.

"Oh, I beg your pardon!" 19.7

"Oh, ich bitte um Verzeihung!"

cried Alice hastily, afraid that she had hurt the poor animal's feelings. 19.8

rief Alice hastig, weil sie fürchtete, die Gefühle des armen Tieres verletzt zu haben.

"I quite forgot you didn't like cats." 19.9

"Ich hatte ganz vergessen, dass du keine Katzen magst."

"Not like cats!" 20.1

"Nicht wie Katzen!"

cried the Mouse, in a shrill, passionate voice. 20.2

rief die Maus mit schriller, leidenschaftlicher Stimme.

20.3 "Would you like cats if you were me?"

"Würdest du Katzen mögen, wenn du an meiner Stelle wärst?"

21.1 "Well, perhaps not," said Alice in a soothing tone:

"Nun, vielleicht nicht," sagte Alice in einem beruhigenden Ton:

21.2 "don't be angry about it.

"Sei nicht böse darüber.

21.3 And yet I wish I could show you our cat Dinah:

Und doch wünschte ich, ich könnte dir unsere Katze Dinah zeigen:

21.4 I think you'd take a fancy to cats if you could only see her.

Ich glaube, du würdest dich in Katzen verlieben, wenn du sie nur sehen könntest.

21.5 She is such a dear quiet thing,"

Sie ist so ein liebes, ruhiges Ding,"

21.6 Alice went on, half to herself, as she swam lazily about in the pool,

fuhr Alice fort, halb zu sich selbst, während sie träge im Teich herumschwamm,

21.7 "and she sits purring so nicely by the fire,

"und sie sitzt so schön schnurrend am Feuer,

21.8 licking her paws and washing her face -

leckt sich die Pfoten und wäscht sich das Gesicht -

21.9 and she is such a nice soft thing to nurse -

und sie ist so ein nettes, weiches Ding, das man stillen kann -

and she's such a capital one for catching mice - oh,   21.10
und sie ist so toll, um Mäuse zu fangen - oh,

I beg your pardon!"   21.11
ich bitte um Verzeihung!"

cried Alice again, for this time the Mouse was   21.12
bristling all over, and she felt certain it must be really
offended.
rief Alice wieder, denn diesmal war die Maus ganz
aufgeregt, und sie fühlte, dass sie wirklich beleidigt sein
musste.

"We won't talk about her any more if you'd rather   21.13
not."
"Wir werden nicht mehr über sie reden, wenn du das nicht
möchtest."

"We indeed!" cried the Mouse,   22.1
"Ja, wir," rief die Maus,

who was trembling down to the end of his tail.   22.2
die bis zum Ende ihres Schwanzes zitterte.

"As if I would talk on such a subject!   22.3
"Als ob ich über so ein Thema sprechen würde!

Our family always hated cats: 22.4
Unsere Familie hat die Katzen immer gehasst:

nasty, low, vulgar things!   22.5
böse, niedere, vulgäre Dinger!

Don't let me hear the name again!"   22.6
Ich will den Namen nicht mehr hören!"

23.1   "I won't indeed!"

"Das werde ich nicht,"

23.2   said Alice, in a great hurry to change the subject of conversation.

sagte Alice, die es sehr eilig hatte, das Gesprächsthema zu wechseln.

23.3   "Are you — are you fond — of — of dogs?"

"Bist du ein Freund von Hunden?"

23.4   The Mouse did not answer, so Alice went on eagerly:

Die Maus antwortete nicht, und so fuhr Alice eifrig fort:

23.5   "There is such a nice little dog near our house I should like to show you!

"In der Nähe unseres Hauses gibt es einen so netten kleinen Hund, den ich dir gerne zeigen möchte!

23.6   A little bright-eyed terrier, you know, with oh, such long curly brown hair!

Ein kleiner helläugiger Terrier, weißt du, mit ach so langem, lockigem, braunem Haar!

23.7   And it'll fetch things when you throw them, and it'll sit up and beg for its dinner, and all sorts of things — I can't remember half of them — and it belongs to a farmer, you know, and he says it's so useful, it's worth a hundred pounds!

Und er apportiert Dinge, wenn man sie wirft, und er setzt sich hin und bettelt um sein Essen, und alles Mögliche — ich kann mich nicht an die Hälfte erinnern — und er gehört einem Bauern, weißt du, und er sagt, er ist so nützlich, dass er hundert Pfund wert ist!

23.8   He says it kills all the rats and — oh dear!"

Er sagt, es tötet alle Ratten und — oh je!"

cried Alice in a sorrowful tone,

23.9

rief Alice in einem traurigen Ton,

"I'm afraid I've offended it again!"

23.10

"ich fürchte, ich habe es wieder beleidigt!"

For the Mouse was swimming away from her as hard as it could go, and making quite a commotion in the pool as it went.

23.11

Denn die Maus schwamm von ihr weg, so schnell sie konnte, und machte dabei einen ziemlichen Aufruhr im Teich.

So she called softly after it, "Mouse dear!

24.1

Also rief sie ihm leise hinterher, "Liebe Maus!

Do come back again, and we won't talk about cats or dogs either, if you don't like them!"

24.2

Komm wieder zurück, und wir werden auch nicht über Katzen oder Hunde reden, wenn du sie nicht magst!"

When the Mouse heard this,

24.3

Als die Maus dies hörte,

it turned round and swam slowly back to her:

24.4

drehte sie sich um und schwamm langsam zu ihr zurück:

its face was quite pale (with passion, Alice thought), and it said in a low trembling voice,

24.5

ihr Gesicht war ganz blass (vor Leidenschaft, dachte Alice), und sie sagte mit leiser, zitternder Stimme,

24.6 "Let us get to the shore, and then I'll tell you my history, and you'll understand why it is I hate cats and dogs."

"Lass uns ans Ufer kommen, und dann werde ich dir meine Geschichte erzählen, und du wirst verstehen, warum ich Katzen und Hunde hasse."

25.1 It was high time to go, for the pool was getting quite crowded with the birds and animals that had fallen into it:

Es war höchste Zeit zu gehen, denn der Teich war schon ziemlich voll mit Vögeln und Tieren, die hineingefallen waren:

25.2 there were a Duck and a Dodo, a Lory and an Eaglet, and several other curious creatures.

eine Ente und ein Dodo, ein Lory und ein Adler und viele andere seltsame Kreaturen.

25.3 Alice led the way, and the whole party swam to the shore.

Alice ging voran, und die ganze Gruppe schwamm zum Ufer.

CHAPTER III. A Caucus-Race and a Long Tale

KAPITEL III. Ein Caucus-Rennen und eine lange Erzählung

1.1   They were indeed a queer-looking party that assembled on the bank -

Es war in der Tat eine seltsam aussehende Gruppe, die sich am Ufer versammelt hatte -

1.2   the birds with draggled feathers, the animals with their fur clinging close to them, and all dripping wet, cross, and uncomfortable.

die Vögel mit zerzausten Federn, die Tiere, deren Fell dicht an ihnen klebte, und alle triefend nass, verärgert und unbehaglich.

2.1   The first question of course was,

Die erste Frage war natürlich,

2.2   how to get dry again:

wie man wieder trocken werden konnte:

they had a consultation about this, and after a few minutes it seemed quite natural to Alice to find herself talking familiarly with them, as if she had known them all her life.

2.3

Sie berieten sich darüber, und nach ein paar Minuten schien es Alice ganz natürlich, dass sie sich mit ihnen so vertraut unterhielt, als ob sie sie schon ihr ganzes Leben lang kennen würde.

Indeed, she had quite a long argument with the Lory, who at last turned sulky, and would only say:

2.4

In der Tat hatte sie einen langen Streit mit dem Lory, der schließlich mürrisch wurde und nur sagte:

"I am older than you, and must know better;"

2.5

"Ich bin älter als du und muss es besser wissen,"

and this Alice would not allow without knowing how old it was, and, as the Lory positively refused to tell its age, there was no more to be said.

2.6

was Alice nicht zulassen wollte, ohne zu wissen, wie alt er war, und da der Lory sich definitiv weigerte, sein Alter zu nennen, gab es nichts mehr zu sagen.

At last the Mouse, who seemed to be a person of authority among them, called out:

3.1

Endlich rief die Maus, die eine Autoritätsperson unter ihnen zu sein schien:

"Sit down, all of you, and listen to me!

3.2

"Setzt euch alle hin und hört mir zu!

I'll soon make you dry enough!"

3.3

Ich werde euch bald trocken genug machen!"

3.4 They all sat down at once, in a large ring, with the Mouse in the middle.

Sie setzten sich alle gleichzeitig in einem großen Kreis, mit der Maus in der Mitte.

3.5 Alice kept her eyes anxiously fixed on it, for she felt sure she would catch a bad cold if she did not get dry very soon.

Alice blickte ängstlich auf sie, denn sie war sich sicher, dass sie sich eine schlimme Erkältung holen würde, wenn sie nicht bald trocken würde.

4.1 "Ahem!" said the Mouse with an important air,

"Ähem!" sagte die Maus mit wichtiger Miene,

4.2 "are you all ready? This is the driest thing I know.

"seid ihr alle bereit? Das ist das Trockenste, was ich kenne.

4.3 Silence all round, if you please!

Ruhe, wenn ich bitten darf!

4.4 'William the Conqueror, whose cause was favoured by the pope, was soon submitted to by the English, who wanted leaders, and had been of late much accustomed to usurpation and conquest.

Wilhelm der Eroberer, dessen Sache vom Papst begünstigt wurde, wurde bald von den Engländern unterworfen, die nach Anführern suchten und in letzter Zeit an Usurpation und Eroberung gewöhnt waren.

4.5 Edwin and Morcar, the earls of Mercia and Northumbria — "'

Edwin und Morcar, die Grafen von Mercia und Northumbria — "

"Ugh!" said the Lory, with a shiver.   5.1
"Igitt!" sagte der Lory mit einem Schauder.

"I beg your pardon!"   6.1
"Ich bitte um Verzeihung!"

said the Mouse, frowning, but very politely: 6.2
sagte die Maus stirnrunzelnd, aber sehr höflich:

"Did you speak?"   6.3
"Hast du gesprochen?"

"Not I!" said the Lory hastily.   7.1
"Ich nicht!" sagte der Lory eilig.

"I thought you did," said the Mouse.   8.1
"Das dachte ich mir schon," sagte die Maus.

" — I proceed.   8.2
"Ich fahre fort.

'Edwin and Morcar, the earls of Mercia and   8.3
Northumbria, declared for him: and even Stigand,
the patriotic archbishop of Canterbury, found it
advisable — "'
Edwin und Morcar, die Grafen von Mercia und
Northumbria, sprachen sich für ihn aus, und selbst
Stigand, der patriotische Erzbischof von Canterbury,
fand es ratsam — "

"Found what?" said the Duck.   9.1
"Was gefunden?" fragte die Ente.

10.1 "Found it," the Mouse replied rather crossly:
"Ich habe es gefunden," antwortete die Maus etwas
verärgert:

10.2 "of course you know what 'it' means."
"Natürlich weißt du, was 'es' bedeutet."

11.1 "I know what 'it' means well enough, when I find a
thing,"
"Ich weiß genau, was 'es' bedeutet, wenn ich etwas finde,"

11.2 said the Duck: "it's generally a frog or a worm.
sagte die Ente, "normalerweise ist es ein Frosch oder ein
Wurm.

11.3 The question is, what did the archbishop find?"
Die Frage ist, was hat der Erzbischof gefunden?"

12.1 The Mouse did not notice this question, but hurriedly
went on,
Die Maus bemerkte diese Frage nicht, sondern fuhr eilig
fort:

12.2 "' — found it advisable to go with Edgar Atheling to
meet William and offer him the crown.
"' — fand es ratsam, mit Edgar Atheling zu William zu
gehen und ihm die Krone anzubieten.

12.3 William's conduct at first was moderate.
William verhielt sich anfangs mäßig.

12.4 But the insolence of his Normans — ' How are you
getting on now,
Aber die Unverschämtheit seiner Normannen — Wie geht
es dir jetzt,

my dear?" it continued, turning to Alice as it spoke. 12.5
meine Liebe?" fuhr sie fort und wandte sich dabei an Alice.

"As wet as ever," said Alice in a melancholy tone: 13.1
"So nass wie immer," sagte Alice in einem
melancholischen Ton:

"it doesn't seem to dry me at all." 13.2
"Es scheint mich überhaupt nicht zu trocknen."

"In that case," said the Dodo solemnly, rising to its 14.1
feet,
"In diesem Fall," sagte der Dodo feierlich und erhob sich,

"I move that the meeting adjourn, 14.2
"beantrage ich die Vertagung der Versammlung,

for the immediate adoption of more energetic 14.3
remedies — "
damit sofort energischere Maßnahmen ergriffen werden
können — "

"Speak English!" said the Eaglet. 15.1
"Sprich Englisch!" sagte das Eaglet.

"I don't know the meaning of half those long words, 15.2
and, what's more, I don't believe you do either!"
"Ich kenne die Bedeutung der Hälfte dieser langen Wörter
nicht, und außerdem glaube ich, dass du sie auch nicht
kennst!"

And the Eaglet bent down its head to hide a smile: 15.3
Und der Adler senkte den Kopf, um ein Lächeln zu
verbergen:

15.4 **some of the other birds tittered audibly.**

einige der anderen Vögel kicherten hörbar.

16.1 **"What I was going to say," said the Dodo in an offended tone,**

"Was ich sagen wollte," sagte der Dodo in beleidigtem Ton,

16.2 **"was, that the best thing to get us dry would be a Caucus- race."**

"war, dass das Beste, um uns trocken zu bekommen, ein Caucus-Rennen wäre."

17.1 **"What is a Caucus-race?" said Alice;**

"Was ist eine Caucus-Rasse?" fragte Alice;

17.2 **not that she wanted much to know, but the Dodo had paused as if it thought that somebody ought to speak, and no one else seemed inclined to say anything.**

nicht dass sie viel wissen wollte, aber der Dodo hatte eine Pause gemacht, als ob er dachte, dass jemand etwas sagen sollte, und niemand sonst schien etwas sagen zu wollen.

18.1 **"Why," said the Dodo,**

"Nun," sagte der Dodo,

18.2 **"the best way to explain it is to do it."**

"der beste Weg, es zu erklären, ist, es zu tun."

18.3 **(And, as you might like to try the thing yourself, some winter day, I will tell you how the Dodo managed it.)**

(Und da du es vielleicht selbst einmal ausprobieren möchtest, werde ich dir an einem Wintertag erzählen, wie der Dodo es geschafft hat.)

First it marked out a race-course, in a sort of circle, ("the exact shape doesn't matter," 19.1

Zuerst wurde eine Rennstrecke in einer Art Kreis abgesteckt ("die genaue Form spielt keine Rolle,"

it said,) and then all the party were placed along the course, here and there. 19.2

hieß es), und dann wurden alle Teilnehmer hier und dort entlang der Strecke platziert.

There was no "One, two, three, and away," 19.3

Es gab kein "Eins, zwei, drei, und los,"

but they began running when they liked, and left off when they liked, so that it was not easy to know when the race was over. 19.4

sondern sie fingen an zu laufen, wann sie wollten, und hörten auf, wann sie wollten, so dass es nicht leicht war, zu wissen, wann das Rennen zu Ende war.

However, when they had been running half an hour or so, and were quite dry again, the Dodo suddenly called out: 19.5

Doch als sie etwa eine halbe Stunde gelaufen und wieder ganz trocken waren, rief der Dodo plötzlich:

"The race is over!" 19.6

"Das Rennen ist vorbei!"

and they all crowded round it, panting, and asking: 19.7

und alle drängten sich keuchend um ihn herum und fragten:

"But who has won?" 19.8

"Aber wer hat gewonnen?"

20.1 This question the Dodo could not answer without a great deal of thought, and it sat for a long time with one finger pressed upon its forehead (the position in which you usually see Shakespeare, in the pictures of him), while the rest waited in silence.

Diese Frage konnte der Dodo nicht ohne langes Nachdenken beantworten und saß lange Zeit mit einem Finger auf der Stirn (die Haltung, in der man Shakespeare auf den Bildern von ihm zu sehen pflegt), während die anderen schweigend warteten.

20.2 At last the Dodo said, "Everybody has won,

Schließlich sagte der Dodo: "Alle haben gewonnen,

20.3 and all must have prizes."

und alle müssen einen Preis bekommen."

21.1 "But who is to give the prizes?"

"Aber wer vergibt die Preise?"

21.2 quite a chorus of voices asked.

fragten viele Stimmen im Chor.

22.1 "Why, she, of course,"

"Sie natürlich,"

22.2 said the Dodo, pointing to Alice with one finger; and the whole party at once crowded round her, calling out in a confused way:

sagte der Dodo und zeigte mit einem Finger auf Alice, und sofort drängte sich die ganze Gesellschaft um sie herum und rief durcheinander:

22.3 "Prizes! Prizes!"

"Preise! Preise!"

Alice had no idea what to do, and in despair she put her hand in her pocket, and pulled out a box of comfits, (luckily the salt water had not got into it), and handed them round as prizes.

23.1

Alice wusste nicht, was sie tun sollte, und in ihrer Verzweiflung griff sie in ihre Tasche und zog eine Schachtel mit Kleidern heraus (zum Glück war das Salzwasser nicht hineingekommen) und verteilte sie als Preise.

There was exactly one a-piece, all round.

23.2

Es gab genau einen pro Stück, für alle.

"But she must have a prize herself, you know," said the Mouse.

24.1

"Aber sie muss doch selbst einen Preis haben," sagte die Maus.

"Of course," the Dodo replied very gravely.

25.1

"Natürlich," antwortete der Dodo sehr ernst.

"What else have you got in your pocket?"

25.2

"Was hast du noch in deiner Tasche?"

he went on, turning to Alice.

25.3

fuhr er fort und wandte sich an Alice.

"Only a thimble," said Alice sadly.

26.1

"Nur ein Fingerhut," sagte Alice traurig.

"Hand it over here," said the Dodo.

27.1

"Gib es her," sagte der Dodo.

28.1 Then they all crowded round her once more, while the Dodo solemnly presented the thimble, saying:

Dann drängten sich alle noch einmal um sie, während der Dodo feierlich den Fingerhut überreichte und sagte:

28.2 "We beg your acceptance of this elegant thimble;"

"Wir bitten Sie, diesen eleganten Fingerhut anzunehmen,"

28.3 and, when it had finished this short speech, they all cheered.

und als er diese kurze Rede beendet hatte, jubelten alle.

29.1 Alice thought the whole thing very absurd, but they all looked so grave that she did not dare to laugh;

Alice fand das Ganze sehr absurd, aber sie sahen alle so ernst aus, dass sie nicht zu lachen wagte;

29.2 and, as she could not think of anything to say, she simply bowed, and took the thimble, looking as solemn as she could.

und da ihr nichts einfiel, verbeugte sie sich einfach und nahm den Fingerhut, wobei sie so ernst wie möglich aussah.

30.1 The next thing was to eat the comfits:

Als Nächstes wurden die Beigaben verspeist:

30.2 this caused some noise and confusion, as the large birds complained that they could not taste theirs, and the small ones choked and had to be patted on the back.

Das verursachte einigen Lärm und Verwirrung, denn die großen Vögel beschwerten sich, dass sie ihre Beigaben nicht schmecken konnten, und die kleinen verschluckten sich und mussten auf den Rücken geklopft werden.

However, it was over at last, and they sat down again in a ring, and begged the Mouse to tell them something more. 30.3

Aber schließlich war es vorbei, und sie setzten sich wieder in einen Ring und baten die Maus, ihnen noch etwas zu erzählen.

"You promised to tell me your history, you know," 31.1

"Du hast mir versprochen, mir deine Geschichte zu erzählen,"

said Alice, "and why it is you hate — C and D," 31.2

sagte Alice, "und warum du C und D hasst,"

she added in a whisper, half afraid that it would be offended again. 31.3

fügte sie flüsternd hinzu, halb aus Angst, wieder beleidigt zu werden.

"Mine is a long and a sad tale." 32.1

"Meine Geschichte ist lang und traurig."

said the Mouse, turning to Alice, and sighing. 32.2

sagte die Maus, drehte sich zu Alice um und seufzte.

"It is a long tail, certainly," 33.1

"Ja, es ist ein langer Schwanz,"

said Alice, looking down with wonder at the Mouse's tail; 33.2

sagte Alice und schaute verwundert auf den Schwanz der Maus hinunter;

"but why do you call it sad?" 33.3

"aber warum nennst du ihn traurig?"

33.4 And she kept on puzzling about it while the Mouse was speaking, so that her idea of the tale was something like this: —

Und sie rätselte weiter, während die Maus sprach, so dass ihre Vorstellung von der Geschichte in etwa so aussah

34.1 "Fury said to a mouse, That he met in the house:

"Fury sagte zu einer Maus, die er im Haus traf:

34.2 'Let us both go to law: I will prosecute you.

'Lass uns beide vor Gericht gehen: Ich werde dich anklagen.

34.3 — Come, I'll take no denial; We must have a trial:

Komm, ich will nicht leugnen, wir müssen einen Prozess haben:

34.4 For really this morning I've nothing to do.'

Denn heute Morgen habe ich wirklich nichts zu tun.'

34.5 Said the mouse to the cur,

Sagte die Maus zum Köter:

34.6 'Such a trial, dear sir, With no jury or judge, would be wasting our breath.'

'So ein Prozess, lieber Herr, ohne Geschworene und Richter, wäre reine Zeitverschwendung.'

34.7 'I'll be judge, I'll be jury,'

'Ich bin der Richter, ich bin die Jury,'

34.8 Said cunning old Fury:

sagte der schlaue alte Fury:

'I'll try the whole cause, and condemn you to death."' 34.9
'Ich werde die ganze Sache verhandeln und dich zum Tode verurteilen."'

"You are not attending!" said the Mouse to Alice severely. 35.1
"Du bist nicht anwesend!" sagte die Maus streng zu Alice.

"What are you thinking of?" 35.2
"Woran denkst du denn?"

"I beg your pardon," said Alice very humbly: 36.1
"Ich bitte um Verzeihung," sagte Alice sehr bescheiden:

"you had got to the fifth bend, I think?" 36.2
"Sie waren, glaube ich, bis zur fünften Kurve gekommen?"

"I had not!" cried the Mouse, sharply and very angrily. 37.1
"Ich hatte nicht!" rief die Maus scharf und sehr wütend.

"A knot!" 38.1
"Ein Knoten,"

said Alice, always ready to make herself useful, and looking anxiously about her. 38.2
sagte Alice, die immer bereit war, sich nützlich zu machen, und sich ängstlich umsah.

"Oh, do let me help to undo it!" 38.3
"Oh, lass mich doch helfen, ihn zu lösen!"

"I shall do nothing of the sort," said the Mouse, 39.1
"Ich werde nichts dergleichen tun," sagte die Maus,

39.2 getting up and walking away.
stand auf und ging weg.

39.3 "You insult me by talking such nonsense!"
"Du beleidigst mich, indem du solchen Unsinn redest!"

40.1 "I didn't mean it!" pleaded poor Alice.
"Ich habe es nicht so gemeint!" flehte die arme Alice.

40.2 "But you're so easily offended, you know!"
"Aber du bist so leicht zu kränken, weißt du!"

41.1 The Mouse only growled in reply.
Die Maus knurrte nur zur Antwort.

42.1 "Please come back and finish your story!"
"Komm bitte zurück und beende deine Geschichte!"

42.2 Alice called after it; and the others all joined in chorus,
rief Alice ihr nach, und die anderen stimmten im Chor ein,

42.3 "Yes, please do!"
"Ja, bitte!"

42.4 but the Mouse only shook its head impatiently, and walked a little quicker.
aber die Maus schüttelte nur ungeduldig den Kopf und ging ein wenig schneller.

43.1 "What a pity it wouldn't stay!"
"Schade, dass es nicht bleibt,"

sighed the Lory, as soon as it was quite out of sight; and an old Crab took the opportunity of saying to her daughter:

43.2

seufzte das Lory, sobald es ganz außer Sichtweite war, und eine alte Krabbe nutzte die Gelegenheit, um zu ihrer Tochter zu sagen:

"Ah, my dear!

43.3

"Ach, meine Liebe!

Let this be a lesson to you never to lose your temper!"

43.4

Das soll dir eine Lehre sein, niemals die Beherrschung zu verlieren!"

"Hold your tongue, Ma!"

43.5

"Hüte deine Zunge, Mama,"

said the young Crab, a little snappishly.

43.6

sagte die junge Krabbe ein wenig schnippisch.

"You're enough to try the patience of an oyster!"

43.7

"Du stellst die Geduld einer Auster auf die Probe!"

"I wish I had our Dinah here, I know I do!"

44.1

"Ich wünschte, ich hätte unsere Dinah hier, ich weiß es!"

said Alice aloud, addressing nobody in particular.

44.2

sagte Alice laut, an niemanden gerichtet.

"She'd soon fetch it back!"

44.3

"Sie würde es bald zurückholen!"

"And who is Dinah, if I might venture to ask the question?"

45.1

"Und wer ist Dinah, wenn ich mir die Frage erlauben darf?"

45.2 **said the Lory.**
fragte der Lory.

46.1 **Alice replied eagerly, for she was always ready to talk about her pet:**
Alice antwortete eifrig, denn sie war immer bereit, über ihr Haustier zu sprechen:

46.2 **"Dinah's our cat.**
"Dinah ist unsere Katze.

46.3 **And she's such a capital one for catching mice you can't think!**
Und sie ist so toll im Mäusefangen, dass man gar nicht glauben kann!

46.4 **And oh, I wish you could see her after the birds!**
Und oh, ich wünschte, du könntest sehen, wie sie die Vögel jagt!

46.5 **Why, she'll eat a little bird as soon as look at it!"**
Sie frisst einen kleinen Vogel, sobald sie ihn ansieht!"

47.1 **This speech caused a remarkable sensation among the party.**
Diese Rede erregte in der Gruppe großes Aufsehen.

47.2 **Some of the birds hurried off at once: one old Magpie began wrapping itself up very carefully, remarking:**
Einige der Vögel eilten sofort davon: eine alte Elster begann, sich sehr sorgfältig einzuwickeln und bemerkte:

47.3 **"I really must be getting home;**
"Ich muss wirklich nach Hause;

the night-air doesn't suit my throat!"   47.4
die Nachtluft ist nicht gut für meine Kehle!"

and a Canary called out in a trembling voice to its   47.5
children:
und ein Kanarienvogel rief mit zitternder Stimme seinen
Kindern zu:

"Come away, my dears!   47.6
"Kommt weg, meine Lieben!

It's high time you were all in bed!"   47.7
Es ist höchste Zeit, dass ihr alle ins Bett geht!"

On various pretexts they all moved off,   47.8
Unter verschiedenen Vorwänden zogen sie alle weg,

and Alice was soon left alone.   47.9
und Alice blieb bald allein zurück.

"I wish I hadn't mentioned Dinah!"   48.1
"Ich wünschte, ich hätte Dinah nicht erwähnt,"

she said to herself in a melancholy tone.   48.2
sagte sie zu sich selbst in einem melancholischen Ton.

"Nobody seems to like her, down here, and I'm sure   48.3
she's the best cat in the world!
"Niemand scheint sie hier zu mögen, und ich bin sicher,
dass sie die beste Katze der Welt ist!

Oh, my dear Dinah!   48.4
Ach, meine liebe Dinah!

I wonder if I shall ever see you any more!"   48.5
Ich frage mich, ob ich dich jemals wiedersehen werde!"

48.6 And here poor Alice began to cry again,

Und hier begann die arme Alice wieder zu weinen,

48.7 for she felt very lonely and low-spirited.

denn sie fühlte sich sehr einsam und niedergeschlagen.

48.8 In a little while, however, she again heard a little pattering of footsteps in the distance, and she looked up eagerly, half hoping that the Mouse had changed his mind, and was coming back to finish his story.

Nach einer Weile hörte sie jedoch wieder Schritte in der Ferne, und sie blickte eifrig auf, halb in der Hoffnung, dass die Maus es sich anders überlegt hatte und zurückkam, um ihre Geschichte zu beenden.

CHAPTER IV. The Rabbit Sends in a Little Bill

KAPITEL IV. Das Kaninchen schickt eine kleine Rechnung ein

1.1 It was the White Rabbit, trotting slowly back again, and looking anxiously about as it went, as if it had lost something; and she heard it muttering to itself:
Es war das weiße Kaninchen, das langsam zurücktrabte und sich dabei ängstlich umsah, als hätte es etwas verloren, und sie hörte es vor sich hinmurmeln:

1.2 "The Duchess! The Duchess! Oh my dear paws!
"Die Herzogin! Die Herzogin! Ach, meine lieben Pfoten!

1.3 Oh my fur and whiskers!
Oh, mein Fell und meine Schnurrhaare!

1.4 She'll get me executed,
Sie wird mich hinrichten lassen,

1.5 as sure as ferrets are ferrets!
so sicher wie Frettchen Frettchen sind!

1.6 Where can I have dropped them, I wonder?"
Wo kann ich sie nur verloren haben?"

Alice guessed in a moment that it was looking for
the fan and the pair of white kid gloves, and she very
good-naturedly began hunting about for them, but
they were nowhere to be seen -

1.7

Alice ahnte sofort, dass es den Fächer und die weißen
Ziegenhandschuhe suchte, und sie machte sich gutmütig
auf die Suche danach, aber sie waren nirgends zu sehen -

everything seemed to have changed since her swim in
the pool, and the great hall, with the glass table and
the little door, had vanished completely.

1.8

alles schien sich seit ihrem Bad im Pool verändert zu haben,
und die große Halle mit dem Glastisch und der kleinen Tür
war völlig verschwunden.

Very soon the Rabbit noticed Alice, as she went
hunting about, and called out to her in an angry
tone:

2.1

Schon bald bemerkte das Kaninchen Alice, als sie auf der
Jagd war, und rief ihr in zornigem Ton zu:

"Why, Mary Ann, what are you doing out here?

2.2

"Mary Ann, was machst du denn hier draußen?

Run home this moment, and fetch me a pair of gloves
and a fan!

2.3

Lauf sofort nach Hause und hol mir ein Paar Handschuhe
und einen Fächer!

Quick, now!"

2.4

Schnell, jetzt!"

2.5 **And Alice was so much frightened that she ran off at once in the direction it pointed to, without trying to explain the mistake it had made.**

Und Alice erschrak so sehr, dass sie sofort in die Richtung lief, in die es zeigte, ohne zu versuchen, den Fehler zu erklären, den es gemacht hatte.

3.1 **"He took me for his housemaid,"**

"Er hat mich für sein Hausmädchen gehalten,"

3.2 **she said to herself as she ran.**

sagte sie zu sich selbst, während sie lief.

3.3 **"How surprised he'll be when he finds out who I am!**

"Wie wird er sich wundern, wenn er erfährt, wer ich bin!

3.4 **But I'd better take him his fan and gloves -**

Aber ich bringe ihm besser seinen Fächer und seine Handschuhe -

3.5 **that is, if I can find them."**

wenn ich sie finde."

3.6 **As she said this, she came upon a neat little house, on the door of which was a bright brass plate with the name**

Während sie dies sagte, kam sie an einem hübschen kleinen Haus vorbei, an dessen Tür ein glänzendes Messingschild mit dem Namen

3.7 **"W. RABBIT," engraved upon it.**

"W. RABBIT" eingraviert war.

She went in without knocking, and hurried upstairs, in great fear lest she should meet the real Mary Ann, and be turned out of the house before she had found the fan and gloves.

3.8

Sie ging hinein, ohne anzuklopfen, und eilte die Treppe hinauf, in großer Angst, der echten Mary Ann zu begegnen und aus dem Haus gewiesen zu werden, bevor sie den Fächer und die Handschuhe gefunden hatte.

"How queer it seems," Alice said to herself,

4.1

"Wie seltsam," sagte Alice zu sich selbst,

"to be going messages for a rabbit!

4.2

"einem Kaninchen Nachrichten zu überbringen!

I suppose Dinah'll be sending me on messages next!"

4.3

Ich nehme an, Dinah wird mir als nächstes Nachrichten schicken!"

And she began fancying the sort of thing that would happen:

4.4

Und sie begann sich auszumalen, was dann passieren würde:

"'Miss Alice!

4.5

"'Miss Alice!

Come here directly, and get ready for your walk!'

4.6

Kommen Sie sofort her und machen Sie sich fertig für Ihren Spaziergang!'

'Coming in a minute, nurse!

4.7

'Ich komme gleich, Schwester!

But I've got to see that the mouse doesn't get out.'

4.8

Aber ich muss aufpassen, dass die Maus nicht rauskommt.'

4.9 Only I don't think," Alice went on,

Ich glaube nur nicht," fuhr Alice fort,

4.10 "that they'd let Dinah stop in the house if it began ordering people about like that!"

"dass sie Dinah im Haus halten lassen würden, wenn sie anfängt, die Leute so herumzukommandieren!"

5.1 By this time she had found her way into a tidy little room with a table in the window,

Inzwischen war sie in ein ordentliches kleines Zimmer mit einem Tisch am Fenster gelangt,

5.2 and on it (as she had hoped) a fan and two or three pairs of tiny white kid gloves:

auf dem (wie sie gehofft hatte) ein Fächer und zwei oder drei Paar winzige weiße Ziegenhandschuhe standen:

5.3 she took up the fan and a pair of the gloves, and was just going to leave the room, when her eye fell upon a little bottle that stood near the looking-glass.

Sie nahm den Fächer und ein Paar der Handschuhe und wollte gerade das Zimmer verlassen, als ihr Blick auf eine kleine Flasche fiel, die neben dem Spiegel stand.

5.4 There was no label this time with the words "DRINK ME,"

Diesmal fehlte das Etikett mit der Aufschrift "DRINK ME,"

5.5 but nevertheless she uncorked it and put it to her lips.

aber trotzdem entkorkte sie es und setzte es an ihre Lippen.

5.6 "I know something interesting is sure to happen,"

"Ich weiß, dass immer etwas Interessantes passiert,"

she said to herself, "whenever I eat or drink
anything;

5.7

sagte sie zu sich selbst, "wenn ich etwas esse oder trinke;

so I'll just see what this bottle does.

5.8

also werde ich einfach sehen, was diese Flasche bewirkt.

I do hope it'll make me grow large again, for really
I'm quite tired of being such a tiny little thing!"

5.9

Ich hoffe, dass ich dadurch wieder groß werde, denn ich
habe es wirklich satt, so ein winziges Ding zu sein!"

It did so indeed, and much sooner than she had
expected:

6.1

Das geschah in der Tat, und zwar viel schneller, als sie
erwartet hatte:

before she had drunk half the bottle, she found her
head pressing against the ceiling, and had to stoop to
save her neck from being broken.

6.2

Noch bevor sie die Hälfte der Flasche getrunken hatte, stieß
sie mit dem Kopf gegen die Decke und musste sich bücken,
um sich nicht das Genick zu brechen.

She hastily put down the bottle, saying to herself

6.3

Eilig stellte sie die Flasche ab und sagte zu sich selbst:

"That's quite enough - I hope I shan't grow any more -

6.4

"Das ist genug - ich hoffe, ich werde nicht noch mehr -

As it is, I can't get out at the door -

6.5

so wie es ist, kann ich nicht zur Tür hinausgehen -

I do wish I hadn't drunk quite so much!"

6.6

ich wünschte, ich hätte nicht so viel getrunken!"

7.1 Alas! it was too late to wish that! She went on growing, and growing, and very soon had to kneel down on the floor: in another minute there was not even room for this, and she tried the effect of lying down with one elbow against the door, and the other arm curled round her head.

Leider war es zu spät, sich das zu wünschen! Sie wuchs und wuchs, und bald musste sie sich auf den Boden knien; in einer weiteren Minute war nicht einmal mehr dafür Platz, und sie versuchte es, indem sie sich mit einem Ellbogen gegen die Tür legte und den anderen Arm um den Kopf schlang.

7.2 Still she went on growing, and, as a last resource, she put one arm out of the window, and one foot up the chimney, and said to herself:

Doch sie wuchs weiter, und als letzten Ausweg streckte sie einen Arm aus dem Fenster und einen Fuß in den Schornstein und sagte zu sich selbst:

7.3 "Now I can do no more, whatever happens.

"Jetzt kann ich nichts mehr tun, egal was passiert.

7.4 What will become of me?"

Was wird aus mir werden?"

8.1 Luckily for Alice, the little magic bottle had now had its full effect, and she grew no larger:

Zum Glück für Alice hatte die kleine Zauberflasche nun ihre volle Wirkung entfaltet, und sie wurde nicht größer:

still it was very uncomfortable, and, as there seemed
to be no sort of chance of her ever getting out of the
room again, no wonder she felt unhappy.

8.2

Trotzdem war es sehr unangenehm, und da es keine
Chance zu geben schien, jemals wieder aus dem Zimmer
zu kommen, war es kein Wunder, dass sie sich unglücklich
fühlte.

"It was much pleasanter at home," thought poor
Alice,

9.1

"Zu Hause war es viel angenehmer," dachte die arme Alice,

"when one wasn't always growing larger and smaller,
and being ordered about by mice and rabbits.

9.2

"als man nicht ständig größer und kleiner wurde und von
Mäusen und Kaninchen herumkommandiert wurde.

I almost wish I hadn't gone down that rabbit- hole -

9.3

Ich wünschte fast, ich wäre nicht in den Kaninchenbau
gegangen -

and yet - and yet -

9.4

und doch - und doch -

it's rather curious, you know, this sort of life!

9.5

es ist schon merkwürdig, so ein Leben!

I do wonder what can have happened to me!

9.6

Ich frage mich, was aus mir geworden ist!

When I used to read fairy-tales, I fancied that kind
of thing never happened, and now here I am in the
middle of one!

9.7

Als ich früher Märchen gelesen habe, dachte ich, so etwas
würde nie passieren, und jetzt bin ich mitten in einem
solchen!

9.8 **There ought to be a book written about me, that there ought!**
Es sollte ein Buch über mich geschrieben werden, das sollte es!

9.9 **And when I grow up, I'll write one -**
Und wenn ich erwachsen bin, werde ich eins schreiben -

9.10 **but I'm grown up now,"**
aber ich bin jetzt erwachsen, "

9.11 **she added in a sorrowful tone;**
fügte sie in einem traurigen Tonfall hinzu;

9.12 **"at least there's no room to grow up any more here."**
"zumindest ist hier kein Platz mehr zum Erwachsenwerden."

10.1 **"But then," thought Alice,**
"Aber dann," dachte Alice,

10.2 **"shall I never get any older than I am now?**
"soll ich nie älter werden als jetzt?

10.3 **That'll be a comfort, one way - never to be an old woman -**
Das wäre einerseits ein Trost - nie eine alte Frau zu sein -

10.4 **but then - always to have lessons to learn! Oh,**
aber andererseits - immer Lektionen lernen zu müssen! Oh,

10.5 **I shouldn't like that!"**
das würde mir nicht gefallen!"

11.1 **"Oh, you foolish Alice!" she answered herself.**
"Ach, du dumme Alice," antwortete sie sich selbst.

"How can you learn lessons in here?   11.2
"Wie kannst du hier lernen?

Why, there's hardly room for you, and no room at all   11.3
for any lesson- books!"
Es gibt doch kaum Platz für dich und schon gar keinen Platz
für Lehrbücher!"

And so she went on, taking first one side and then   12.1
the other, and making quite a conversation of it
altogether;
Und so ging sie weiter, erst auf der einen, dann auf der
anderen Seite, und unterhielt sich ziemlich gut;

but after a few minutes she heard a voice outside,   12.2
aber nach ein paar Minuten hörte sie draußen eine Stimme
und blieb stehen,

and stopped to listen.   12.3
um zu lauschen.

"Mary Ann! Mary Ann!" said the voice.   13.1
"Mary Ann! Mary Ann!" sagte die Stimme.

"Fetch me my gloves this moment!"   13.2
"Hol mir sofort meine Handschuhe!"

Then came a little pattering of feet on the stairs.   13.3
Dann ertönte ein leises Fußgetrappel auf der Treppe.

13.4 Alice knew it was the Rabbit coming to look for her, and she trembled till she shook the house, quite forgetting that she was now about a thousand times as large as the Rabbit, and had no reason to be afraid of it.

Alice wusste, dass es das Kaninchen war, das nach ihr suchte, und sie zitterte, bis sie das Haus erschütterte, wobei sie ganz vergaß, dass sie jetzt etwa tausendmal so groß war wie das Kaninchen und keinen Grund hatte, sich vor ihm zu fürchten.

14.1 Presently the Rabbit came up to the door,

Bald darauf kam das Kaninchen zur Tür und versuchte,

14.2 and tried to open it;

sie zu öffnen;

14.3 but, as the door opened inwards, and Alice's elbow was pressed hard against it, that attempt proved a failure.

aber da die Tür nach innen aufging und Alices Ellbogen fest dagegen gedrückt wurde, misslang dieser Versuch.

14.4 Alice heard it say to itself:

Alice hörte, wie es zu sich selbst sagte:

14.5 "Then I'll go round and get in at the window."

"Dann gehe ich herum und steige durch das Fenster ein."

15.1 "That you won't!"

"Das wirst du nicht!"

thought Alice, and, after waiting till she fancied   15.2
she heard the Rabbit just under the window, she
suddenly spread out her hand, and made a snatch in
the air.

dachte Alice, und nachdem sie gewartet hatte, bis sie
glaubte, das Kaninchen unter dem Fenster zu hören,
streckte sie plötzlich ihre Hand aus und schnappte in
der Luft.

She did not get hold of anything, but she heard a little   15.3
shriek and a fall, and a crash of broken glass, from
which she concluded that it was just possible it had
fallen into a cucumber-frame, or something of the
sort.

Sie bekam nichts zu fassen, aber sie hörte einen kleinen
Schrei, einen Sturz und das Krachen von zerbrochenem
Glas, woraus sie schloss, dass es vielleicht in einen
Gurkenkasten oder etwas Ähnliches gefallen war.

Next came an angry voice - the Rabbit's - "Pat! Pat!   16.1
Dann kam eine wütende Stimme - die des Kaninchens -
"Pat! Pat!

Where are you?"   16.2
Wo bist du?"

And then a voice she had never heard before,   16.3
Und dann eine Stimme, die sie noch nie zuvor gehört hatte,

"Sure then I'm here! Digging for apples, yer honour!"   16.4
"Ja, ich bin hier! Ich grabe nach Äpfeln, Euer Ehren!"

"Digging for apples, indeed!" said the Rabbit angrily.   17.1
"Nach Äpfeln graben, ja!" sagte der Hase ärgerlich.

"Here! Come and help me out of this!"   17.2
"Hier! Komm und hilf mir da raus!"

17.3 (Sounds of more broken glass.)
(Geräusche von noch mehr zerbrochenem Glas.)

18.1 "Now tell me, Pat, what's that in the window?"
"Und jetzt sag mir, Pat, was ist das da im Fenster?"

19.1 "Sure, it's an arm, yer honour!" (He pronounced it,
"Sicher, es ist ein Arm, Euer Ehren!" (Er sprach es aus,

19.2 "arrum. ")
"arrum. ")

20.1 "An arm, you goose! Who ever saw one that size?
"Ein Arm, du Gans! Wer hat je einen so großen gesehen?

20.2 Why, it fills the whole window!"
Der füllt ja das ganze Fenster aus!"

21.1 "Sure, it does, yer honour: but it's an arm for all that."
"Ja, das stimmt, Euer Ehren, aber dafür ist es ein Arm."

22.1 "Well, it's got no business there, at any rate:
"Da hat es jedenfalls nichts zu suchen:

22.2 go and take it away!"
Geh und nimm es weg!"

23.1 There was a long silence after this, and Alice could only hear whispers now and then; such as,
Danach herrschte eine lange Stille, und Alice konnte nur hin und wieder ein Flüstern hören, wie:

"Sure, I don't like it, yer honour, at all, at all!"   23.2
"Das gefällt mir gar nicht, Euer Ehren, ganz und gar nicht!"

"Do as I tell you, you coward!"   23.3
"Tu, was ich dir sage, du Feigling!"

and at last she spread out her hand again, and made   23.4
another snatch in the air.
und schließlich streckte sie wieder die Hand aus und
machte einen weiteren Satz in die Luft.

This time there were two little shrieks, and more   23.5
sounds of broken glass.
Diesmal gab es zwei kleine Schreie und weitere Geräusche
von zerbrochenem Glas.

"What a number of cucumber-frames there must be!"   23.6
"Was für eine Anzahl von Gurkenrahmen muss es sein,"

thought Alice.   23.7
dachte Alice.

"I wonder what they'll do next!   23.8
"Ich frage mich, was sie als nächstes tun werden!

As for pulling me out of the window, I only wish they   23.9
could!
Ich wünschte, sie könnten mich aus dem Fenster ziehen!

I'm sure I don't want to stay in here any longer!"   23.10
Ich bin mir sicher, dass ich nicht länger hier drin bleiben
möchte!"

She waited for some time without hearing anything   24.1
more:
Sie wartete einige Zeit, ohne noch etwas zu hören:

24.2 **at last came a rumbling of little cartwheels,**
endlich hörte sie ein Rumpeln und das Geräusch von vielen Stimmen,

24.3 **and the sound of a good many voices all talking together:**
die sich miteinander unterhielten:

24.4 **she made out the words: "Where's the other ladder?**
sie konnte die Worte verstehen: "Wo ist die andere Leiter?

24.5 **– Why, I hadn't to bring but one; Bill's got the other -**
– Warum, Ich musste nur eine mitnehmen; Bill hat die andere -

24.6 **Bill! fetch it here, lad! - Here, put 'em up at this corner -**
Bill! Hol sie her, Junge! - Hier, häng sie an dieser Ecke auf -

24.7 **No, tie 'em together first -**
Nein, binde sie erst zusammen -

24.8 **they don't reach half high enough yet - Oh!**
Sie sind noch nicht hoch genug - Oh!

24.9 **they'll do well enough; don't be particular - Here,**
Sie werden es schon schaffen; sei nicht so wählerisch - Hier,

24.10 **Bill! catch hold of this rope - Will the roof bear?**
Bill! Halt dich an diesem Seil fest - Hält das Dach?

24.11 **– Mind that loose slate - Oh, it's coming down!**
– Pass auf den losen Schiefer auf - Oh, es kommt runter!

24.12 **Heads below!" (a loud crash) - "Now, who did that?**
Köpfe runter!" (ein lautes Krachen) - "Wer war das denn?

– It was Bill, I fancy -   24.13
– Das war Bill, dachte ich mir -

Who's to go down the chimney? - Nay,   24.14
Wer soll den Schornstein hinuntergehen? - Nein,

I shan't! You do it! - That I won't, then!   24.15
das werde ich nicht! Mach du es! - Das werde ich nicht!

– Bill's to go down - Here, Bill!   24.16
– Bill wird untergehen - Hier, Bill!

the master says you're to go down the chimney!"   24.17
Der Meister sagt, du sollst den Schornstein
hinuntergehen!"

"Oh! So Bill's got to come down the chimney, has he?"   25.1
"Oh! Bill muss also den Schornstein hinunterkommen,
was?"

said Alice to herself. "Shy,   25.2
sagte Alice zu sich selbst. "Schüchtern,

they seem to put everything upon Bill!   25.3
sie scheinen alles auf Bill zu schieben!

I wouldn't be in Bill's place for a good deal: 25.4
Ich würde nur ungern an Bills Stelle sein:

this fireplace is narrow, to be sure; but I think I can   25.5
kick a little!"
dieser Kamin ist zwar eng, aber ich glaube, ich kann ein
bisschen treten!"

26.1 She drew her foot as far down the chimney as she could, and waited till she heard a little animal (she couldn't guess of what sort it was) scratching and scrambling about in the chimney close above her:

Sie zog ihren Fuß so weit wie möglich in den Schornstein hinein und wartete, bis sie ein kleines Tierchen (sie konnte nicht erraten, um welche Art es sich handelte) hörte, das im Schornstein dicht über ihr herumscharrte und krabbelte:

26.2 then, saying to herself "This is Bill,"

dann sagte sie zu sich selbst "Das ist Bill,"

26.3 she gave one sharp kick,

gab ihm einen kräftigen Tritt und wartete ab,

26.4 and waited to see what would happen next.

was als Nächstes passieren würde.

27.1 The first thing she heard was a general chorus of

Das erste, was sie hörte, war ein allgemeines

27.2 "There goes Bill!" then the Rabbit's voice along — "Catch him,

"Da ist Bill!" dann die Stimme des Kaninchens: "Fangt ihn,

27.3 you by the hedge!"

ihr da an der Hecke!"

27.4 then silence, and then another confusion of voices — "Hold up his head — Brandy now — Don't choke him — How was it, old fellow?

dann Stille und dann wieder ein Stimmengewirr: "Haltet seinen Kopf hoch, Randy, nicht erwürgen, wie war's, alter Freund?

What happened to you? Tell us all about it!"

27.5

Was ist mit dir passiert? Erzähl uns alles darüber!"

Last came a little feeble, squeaking voice, ("That's
Bill,"

28.1

Zuletzt kam eine kleine, schwache, quietschende Stimme
("Das ist Bill,"

thought Alice,)

28.2

dachte Alice):

"Well, I hardly know — No more, thank ye; I'm better
now — but I'm a deal too flustered to tell you — all I
know is, something comes at me like a Jack-in-the-
box, and up I goes like a sky- rocket!"

28.3

"Nun, ich weiß nicht mehr, danke, mir geht es jetzt besser,
aber ich bin viel zu aufgeregt, um es euch zu sagen - alles,
was ich weiß, ist, dass etwas auf mich zukommt wie ein
Springteufel, und ich fliege hoch wie eine Rakete!"

"So you did, old fellow!" said the others.

29.1

"Das hast du, alter Knabe!" sagten die anderen.

"We must burn the house down!"

30.1

"Wir müssen das Haus niederbrennen,"

said the Rabbit's voice; and Alice called out as loud as
she could,

30.2

sagte die Stimme des Kaninchens, und Alice rief so laut sie
konnte,

"If you do, I'll set Dinah at you!"

30.3

"Wenn du das tust, werde ich Dinah auf dich hetzen!"

31.1 There was a dead silence instantly, and Alice thought to herself:

Sofort herrschte Totenstille, und Alice dachte bei sich:

31.2 "I wonder what they will do next!

"Ich frage mich, was sie als Nächstes tun werden!

31.3 If they had any sense, they'd take the roof off."

Wenn sie vernünftig wären, würden sie das Dach abnehmen."

31.4 After a minute or two, they began moving about again, and Alice heard the Rabbit say:

Nach ein oder zwei Minuten fingen sie wieder an, sich zu bewegen, und Alice hörte das Kaninchen sagen:

31.5 "A barrowful will do, to begin with."

"Für den Anfang reicht eine Grube."

32.1 "A barrowful of what?"

"Was für ein Gerümpel?"

32.2 thought Alice; but she had not long to doubt, for the next moment a shower of little pebbles came rattling in at the window, and some of them hit her in the face.

dachte Alice, aber sie hatte nicht lange Zeit zu zweifeln, denn im nächsten Moment prasselte ein Regen von kleinen Kieselsteinen zum Fenster herein, und einige davon trafen sie im Gesicht.

32.3 "I'll put a stop to this,"

"Ich werde dem ein Ende setzen,"

32.4 she said to herself, and shouted out:

sagte sie zu sich selbst und rief:

"You'd better not do that again!" 32.5

"Das machst du besser nicht noch einmal!"

which produced another dead silence. 32.6

woraufhin wieder Totenstille herrschte.

Alice noticed with some surprise that the pebbles 33.1
were all turning into little cakes as they lay on the
floor, and a bright idea came into her head.

Alice stellte erstaunt fest, dass sich die Kieselsteine, die auf
dem Boden lagen, alle in kleine Kuchen verwandelten, und
ihr kam eine glänzende Idee in den Sinn.

"If I eat one of these cakes," she thought, 33.2

"Wenn ich einen dieser Kuchen esse," dachte sie,

"it's sure to make some change in my size; 33.3

"wird sich meine Größe sicher ändern;

and as it can't possibly make me larger, it must make 33.4
me smaller, I suppose."

und da ich unmöglich größer werden kann, muss ich wohl
kleiner werden."

So she swallowed one of the cakes, 34.1

Also schluckte sie einen der Kuchen und stellte zu ihrer
Freude fest,

and was delighted to find that she began shrinking 34.2
directly.

dass sie sofort zu schrumpfen begann.

34.3 As soon as she was small enough to get through the door, she ran out of the house, and found quite a crowd of little animals and birds waiting outside.

Sobald sie klein genug war, um durch die Tür zu kommen, rannte sie aus dem Haus und fand draußen eine ganze Schar von kleinen Tieren und Vögeln warten.

34.4 The poor little Lizard, Bill, was in the middle, being held up by two guinea-pigs, who were giving it something out of a bottle.

Die arme kleine Eidechse Bill stand in der Mitte und wurde von zwei Meerschweinchen festgehalten, die ihr etwas aus einer Flasche gaben.

34.5 They all made a rush at Alice the moment she appeared; but she ran off as hard as she could, and soon found herself safe in a thick wood.

Sie alle stürzten sich auf Alice, sobald sie auftauchte, aber sie rannte davon, so schnell sie konnte, und fand sich bald in einem dichten Wald in Sicherheit.

35.1 "The first thing I've got to do,"

"Das Erste, was ich tun muss,"

35.2 said Alice to herself, as she wandered about in the wood,

sagte Alice zu sich selbst, während sie im Wald umherwanderte,

35.3 "is to grow to my right size again;

"ist, wieder auf die richtige Größe zu kommen;

35.4 and the second thing is to find my way into that lovely garden.

und das Zweite ist, den Weg in diesen schönen Garten zu finden.

I think that will be the best plan."

35.5

Ich glaube, das wird der beste Plan sein."

It sounded an excellent plan, no doubt, and very neatly and simply arranged;

36.1

Es klang zweifellos nach einem ausgezeichneten Plan, der sehr ordentlich und einfach ausgeführt war;

the only difficulty was, that she had not the smallest idea how to set about it;

36.2

die einzige Schwierigkeit bestand darin, dass sie nicht die geringste Ahnung hatte, wie sie es anstellen sollte;

and while she was peering about anxiously among the trees,

36.3

und während sie ängstlich zwischen den Bäumen herumspähte,

a little sharp bark just over her head made her look up in a great hurry.

36.4

ließ ein kleines scharfes Bellen direkt über ihrem Kopf sie eilig aufblicken.

An enormous puppy was looking down at her with large round eyes, and feebly stretching out one paw, trying to touch her.

37.1

Ein riesiger Welpe schaute mit großen runden Augen auf sie herab und streckte zaghaft eine Pfote aus, um sie zu berühren.

"Poor little thing."

37.2

"Armes kleines Ding."

said Alice, in a coaxing tone, and she tried hard to whistle to it;

37.3

sagte Alice in einem beschwichtigenden Ton, und sie bemühte sich, ihm zu pfeifen;

37.4 but she was terribly frightened all the time at the thought that it might be hungry, in which case it would be very likely to eat her up in spite of all her coaxing.

aber sie hatte die ganze Zeit schreckliche Angst bei dem Gedanken, dass es hungrig sein könnte, und in diesem Fall würde es sie sehr wahrscheinlich auffressen, trotz all ihres Zuredens.

38.1 Hardly knowing what she did, she picked up a little bit of stick, and held it out to the puppy;

Kaum wußte sie, was sie tat, hob sie ein Stöckchen auf und hielt es dem Hündchen hin;

38.2 whereupon the puppy jumped into the air off all its feet at once, with a yelp of delight, and rushed at the stick, and made believe to worry it;

da sprang das Hündchen mit einem Freudengekläff in die Luft, stürzte sich auf das Stöckchen und glaubte, es zu beunruhigen;

38.3 then Alice dodged behind a great thistle,

dann wich Alice hinter eine große Distel aus,

38.4 to keep herself from being run over;

um nicht überfahren zu werden;

38.5 and the moment she appeared on the other side, the puppy made another rush at the stick, and tumbled head over heels in its hurry to get hold of it;

und als sie auf der anderen Seite erschien, stürzte sich das Hündchen wieder auf das Stöckchen und stürzte in seiner Eile, es zu fassen zu bekommen, Hals über Kopf;

then Alice, thinking it was very like having a game of
play with a cart-horse, and expecting every moment
to be trampled under its feet, ran round the thistle
again;

38.6

Alice dachte, es sei wie ein Spiel mit einem Wagenpferd,
und erwartete jeden Augenblick, von ihm zertrampelt zu
werden, und rannte wieder um die Distel herum;

then the puppy began a series of short charges at the
stick, running a very little way forwards each time
and a long way back, and barking hoarsely all the
while, till at last it sat down a good way off, panting,
with its tongue hanging out of its mouth, and its great
eyes half shut.

38.7

dann begann das Hündchen eine Reihe von kurzen
Angriffen auf den Stock, wobei es jedes Mal ein kleines
Stück vorwärts und ein großes Stück zurücklief und dabei
heiser bellte, bis es sich schließlich in einiger Entfernung
hechelnd niederließ, wobei ihm die Zunge aus dem Maul
hing und seine großen Augen halb geschlossen waren.

This seemed to Alice a good opportunity for making
her escape; so she set off at once, and ran till she was
quite tired and out of breath, and till the puppy's bark
sounded quite faint in the distance.

39.1

Das schien Alice eine gute Gelegenheit zu sein, um zu
fliehen, und so machte sie sich sofort auf den Weg und
rannte, bis sie ganz müde und außer Atem war und das
Bellen des Welpen in der Ferne ganz leise zu hören war.

"And yet what a dear little puppy it was!"

40.1

"Und was für ein liebes Hündchen es doch war,"

said Alice, as she leant against a buttercup to rest
herself, and fanned herself with one of the leaves:

40.2

sagte Alice, als sie sich an eine Butterblume lehnte, um sich
auszuruhen, und sich mit einem der Blätter fächelte:

40.3 "I should have liked teaching it tricks very much,
"Ich hätte ihm sehr gerne Kunststücke beigebracht,

40.4 if — if I'd only been the right size to do it! Oh dear!
wenn ich nur die richtige Größe dafür gehabt hätte! Oh je!

40.5 I'd nearly forgotten that I've got to grow up again!
Ich hatte fast vergessen, dass ich wieder erwachsen werden muss!

40.6 Let me see — how is it to be managed?
Mal sehen, wie soll ich das schaffen?

40.7 I suppose I ought to eat or drink something or other;
Ich sollte wohl etwas essen oder trinken;

40.8 but the great question is, what?"
aber die große Frage ist, was?"

41.1 The great question certainly was, what?
Die große Frage war natürlich, was?

41.2 Alice looked all round her at the flowers and the blades of grass, but she did not see anything that looked like the right thing to eat or drink under the circumstances.
Alice schaute um sich herum auf die Blumen und Grashalme, aber sie sah nichts, was unter den gegebenen Umständen das Richtige zum Essen oder Trinken war.

There was a large mushroom growing near her, about   41.3
the same height as herself; and when she had looked
under it, and on both sides of it, and behind it, it
occurred to her that she might as well look and see
what was on the top of it.

In ihrer Nähe wuchs ein großer Pilz, der ungefähr so groß
war wie sie selbst, und als sie darunter, auf beiden Seiten
und dahinter geschaut hatte, kam ihr der Gedanke, dass sie
auch nachsehen könnte, was sich oben auf dem Pilz befand.

She stretched herself up on tiptoe, and peeped over   42.1
the edge of the mushroom, and her eyes immediately
met those of a large blue caterpillar, that was sitting
on the top with its arms folded, quietly smoking a
long hookah, and taking not the smallest notice of
her or of anything else.

Sie stellte sich auf die Zehenspitzen und spähte über den
Rand des Pilzes, und ihre Augen trafen sofort auf die einer
großen blauen Raupe, die mit verschränkten Armen auf der
Spitze saß, in aller Ruhe eine lange Wasserpfeife rauchte
und weder sie noch sonst etwas beachtete.

CHAPTER V. Advice from a Caterpillar

KAPITEL V. Ratschläge von einer Raupe

1.1 The Caterpillar and Alice looked at each other for some time in silence: at last the Caterpillar took the hookah out of its mouth, and addressed her in a languid, sleepy voice.

Die Raupe und Alice sahen sich eine Weile schweigend an, dann nahm die Raupe die Wasserpfeife aus dem Mund und wandte sich mit müder, schläfriger Stimme an sie.

2.1 "Who are you?" said the Caterpillar.

"Wer bist du?" fragte die Raupe.

3.1 This was not an encouraging opening for a conversation.

Das war kein ermutigender Anfang für ein Gespräch.

3.2 Alice replied, rather shyly,

Alice antwortete etwas schüchtern:

"I — I hardly know, sir, just at present — at least I know who I was when I got up this morning, but I think I must have been changed several times since then."

3.3

"Ich weiß es kaum, Sir, nur im Moment - zumindest weiß ich, wer ich war, als ich heute Morgen aufgestanden bin, aber ich glaube, ich muss mich seitdem mehrmals verändert haben."

"What do you mean by that?" said the Caterpillar sternly.

4.1

"Was meinst du damit?" fragte die Raupe streng.

"Explain yourself!"

4.2

"Erkläre dich!"

"I can't explain myself, I'm afraid, sir," said Alice,

5.1

"Ich kann mich leider nicht erklären, Sir," sagte Alice,

"because I'm not myself, you see."

5.2

"denn ich bin nicht ich selbst, wie Sie sehen."

"I don't see," said the Caterpillar.

6.1

"Ich verstehe nicht," sagte die Raupe.

"I'm afraid I can't put it more clearly,"

7.1

"Ich fürchte, deutlicher kann ich es nicht ausdrücken,"

Alice replied very politely,

7.2

antwortete Alice sehr höflich,

7.3 "for I can't understand it myself to begin with; and being so many different sizes in a day is very confusing."

"denn ich kann es selbst nicht verstehen, und so viele verschiedene Größen an einem Tag zu haben, ist sehr verwirrend."

8.1 "It isn't," said the Caterpillar.

"Ist es nicht," sagte die Raupe.

9.1 "Well, perhaps you haven't found it so yet,"

"Nun, vielleicht hast du es noch nicht so empfunden,"

9.2 said Alice;

sagte Alice;

9.3 "but when you have to turn into a chrysalis -

"aber wenn du dich in eine Puppe verwandeln musst -

9.4 you will some day, you know -

das wirst du eines Tages, weißt du -

9.5 and then after that into a butterfly, I should think you'll feel it a little queer, won't you?"

und danach in einen Schmetterling, dann wirst du es wohl ein bisschen komisch finden, nicht wahr?"

10.1 "Not a bit," said the Caterpillar.

"Kein bisschen," sagte die Raupe.

11.1 "Well, perhaps your feelings may be different," said Alice;

"Nun, vielleicht empfindest du das anders," sagte Alice,

"all I know is,   11.2
"ich weiß nur,

it would feel very queer to me."   11.3
dass es sich für mich sehr seltsam anfühlen würde."

"You!" said the Caterpillar contemptuously. "Who   12.1
are you?"
"Du!" sagte die Raupe verächtlich. "Wer bist du?"

Which brought them back again to the beginning of   13.1
the conversation.
Damit waren sie wieder am Anfang des Gesprächs
angelangt.

Alice felt a little irritated at the Caterpillar's making   13.2
such very short remarks, and she drew herself up and
said, very gravely,
Alice fühlte sich ein wenig irritiert, dass die Raupe so kurze
Bemerkungen machte, und sie richtete sich auf und sagte
sehr ernst:

"I think, you ought to tell me who you are, first."   13.3
"Ich denke, du solltest mir zuerst sagen, wer du bist."

"Why?" said the Caterpillar.   14.1
"Warum?" fragte die Raupe.

Here was another puzzling question; and as Alice   15.1
could not think of any good reason, and as the
Caterpillar seemed to be in a very unpleasant state
of mind, she turned away.
Das war eine weitere rätselhafte Frage, und da Alice
kein guter Grund einfiel und die Raupe in einem sehr
unangenehmen Zustand zu sein schien, wandte sie sich ab.

16.1   "Come back!" the Caterpillar called after her.
"Komm zurück!" rief die Raupe ihr nach.

16.2   "I've something important to say!"
"Ich habe etwas Wichtiges zu sagen!"

17.1   This sounded promising, certainly:
Das hörte sich auf jeden Fall vielversprechend an:

17.2   Alice turned and came back again.
Alice drehte sich um und kam wieder zurück.

18.1   "Keep your temper," said the Caterpillar.
"Beherrsche dich," sagte die Raupe.

19.1   "Is that all?"
"Ist das alles?"

19.2   said Alice, swallowing down her anger as well as she could.
sagte Alice und schluckte ihre Wut so gut sie konnte hinunter.

20.1   "No," said the Caterpillar.
"Nein," sagte die Raupe.

21.1   Alice thought she might as well wait, as she had nothing else to do, and perhaps after all it might tell her something worth hearing.
Alice dachte, dass sie genauso gut warten könnte, da sie nichts anderes zu tun hatte, und vielleicht würde es ihr ja doch etwas erzählen, was sie hören wollte.

For some minutes it puffed away without speaking, but at last it unfolded its arms, took the hookah out of its mouth again, and said:

21.2

Einige Minuten lang paffte es, ohne zu sprechen, aber schließlich breitete es die Arme aus, nahm die Wasserpfeife wieder aus dem Mund und sagte:

"So you think you're changed, do you?"

21.3

"Du glaubst also, dass du dich verändert hast?"

"I'm afraid I am, sir," said Alice;

22.1

"Ich fürchte, das bin ich, Sir," sagte Alice;

"I can't remember things as I used -

22.2

"Ich kann mich nicht mehr an Dinge erinnern wie früher -

and I don't keep the same size for ten minutes together!"

22.3

und ich behalte nicht zehn Minuten lang die gleiche Größe!"

"Can't remember what things?"

23.1

"Ich kann mich nicht erinnern, an welche Dinge?"

said the Caterpillar.

23.2

sagte die Raupe.

"Well, I've tried to say,

24.1

"Nun, ich habe versucht,

"How doth the little busy bee,"

24.2

"Wie geht es der kleinen fleißigen Biene"

but it all came different!"

24.3

zu sagen, aber es kam alles anders!"

24.4 **Alice replied in a very melancholy voice.**
antwortete Alice mit einer sehr melancholischen Stimme.

25.1 **"Repeat, "You are old, Father William,"' said the Caterpillar.**
"Wiederhole: "Du bist alt, Vater William," sagte die Raupe.

26.1 **Alice folded her hands, and began:-**
Alice faltete ihre Hände und begann:-

"You are old, Father William," the young man said,	"Sie sind alt, Pater William," sagte der junge Mann,
"And your hair has become very white;	"Und dein Haar ist sehr weiß geworden;
And yet you incessantly stand on your head — .	Und doch stehst du unaufhörlich auf deinem Kopf.
Do you think, at your age, it is right?"	Halten Sie das in Ihrem Alter für richtig?"
"In my youth," Father William replied to his son,	"In meiner Jugend," antwortete Vater William seinem Sohn,
"I feared it might injure the brain;	"Ich befürchtete, es könnte das Gehirn verletzen;
But, now that I'm perfectly sure I have none,	Aber jetzt, wo ich mir ganz sicher bin, habe ich keine,

Why, I do it again and again."

Ich tue es immer wieder."

"You are old," said the youth, "as I mentioned before,

"Du bist alt," sagte der Jüngling, "wie ich schon sagte,

And have grown most uncommonly fat;

Und sind ungewöhnlich dick geworden;

Yet you turned a back-somersault in at the door — .

Aber du hast einen Rückwärtssalto durch die Tür gemacht.

Pray, what is the reason of that?"

Bitte, was ist der Grund dafür?"

"In my youth,"

"In meiner Jugend,"

said the sage, as he shook his grey locks,

sagte der Weise, während er seine grauen Locken schüttelte,

"I kept all my limbs very supple

"Ich hielt alle meine Glieder sehr geschmeidig

By the use of this ointment - one shilling the box -

Durch die Verwendung dieser Münze - ein Schilling pro Kiste -

Allow me to sell you a couple?"

Erlauben Sie mir, Ihnen ein paar zu verkaufen?"

"You are old," said the youth,

"Du bist alt," sagte der Jüngling,

"and your jaws are too weak.	"und dein Kiefer ist zu schwach.
For anything tougher than suet;	Für alles, was zäher ist als Talg;
Yet you finished the goose,	Aber du hast die Gans fertig gemacht,
with the bones and the beak — .	mit den Knochen und dem Schnabel.
Pray, how did you manage to do it?"	Bitte, wie haben Sie das geschafft?"
"In my youth," said his father,	"In meiner Jugend," sagte sein Vater,
"I took to the law,	"habe ich mich für das Gesetz entschieden,
And argued each case with my wife;	Und ich habe jeden Fall mit meiner Frau besprochen;
And the muscular strength, which it gave to my jaw,	Und die Muskelkraft, die sie meinem Kiefer verliehen hat,
Has lasted the rest of my life."	Es hat den Rest meines Lebens überdauert."
"You are old," said the youth,	"Du bist alt," sagte der Jüngling,
"one would hardly suppose.	"man würde kaum annehmen, dass du alt bist.

That your eye was as steady as ever;

Dass Ihr Blick so sicher war wie immer;

Yet you balanced an eel on the end of your nose —.

Und doch balancieren Sie einen Aal auf Ihrer Nasenspitze.

What made you so awfully clever?"

Was hat dich so furchtbar klug gemacht?"

"I have answered three questions, and that is enough,"

"Ich habe drei Fragen beantwortet, und das ist genug,"

Said his father; "don't give yourself airs!

Sagte sein Vater: "Mach dir keine Illusionen!

Do you think I can listen all day to such stuff?

Glaubst du, ich kann mir so etwas den ganzen Tag anhören?

Be off, or I'll kick you down stairs!"

Hau ab, sonst trete ich dich die Treppe hinunter!"

"That is not said right," said the Caterpillar.

28.1

"Das ist nicht richtig gesagt," sagte die Raupe.

"Not quite right, I'm afraid," said Alice, timidly;

29.1

"Nicht ganz richtig, fürchte ich," sagte Alice zaghaft;

"some of the words have got altered."

29.2

"einige der Wörter sind verändert worden."

"It is wrong from beginning to end,"

30.1

"Das ist von Anfang bis Ende falsch,"

98

30.2 said the Caterpillar decidedly,
sagte die Raupe entschlossen,

30.3 and there was silence for some minutes.
und es herrschte einige Minuten lang Schweigen.

31.1 The Caterpillar was the first to speak.
Die Raupe ergriff als erste das Wort.

32.1 "What size do you want to be?" it asked.
"Welche Größe willst du haben?" fragte es.

33.1 "Oh, I'm not particular as to size,"
"Oh, ich bin nicht wählerisch, was die Größe angeht,"

33.2 Alice hastily replied;
antwortete Alice hastig,

33.3 "only one doesn't like changing so often, you know."
"man möchte sich nur nicht so oft umziehen, weißt du."

34.1 "I don't know," said the Caterpillar.
"Ich weiß es nicht," sagte die Raupe.

35.1 Alice said nothing:
Alice sagte nichts:

35.2 she had never been so much contradicted in her life
before, and she felt that she was losing her temper.
Sie hatte noch nie in ihrem Leben so viel Widerspruch
erfahren, und sie spürte, dass sie die Beherrschung verlor.

"Are you content now?" said the Caterpillar. 36.1

"Bist du jetzt zufrieden?" fragte die Raupe.

"Well, I should like to be a little larger, sir, if you wouldn't mind," 37.1

"Nun, ich wäre gerne etwas größer, Sir, wenn es Ihnen nichts ausmacht,"

said Alice: "three inches is such a wretched height to be." 37.2

sagte Alice, "drei Zoll sind eine erbärmliche Größe."

"It is a very good height indeed!" 38.1

"Das ist wirklich eine sehr gute Höhe!"

said the Caterpillar angrily, 38.2

sagte die Raupe wütend und richtete sich auf,

rearing itself upright as it spoke (it was exactly three inches high). 38.3

während sie sprach (sie war genau drei Zentimeter hoch).

"But I'm not used to it!" 39.1

"Aber ich bin es nicht gewohnt!"

pleaded poor Alice in a piteous tone. 39.2

flehte die arme Alice in kläglichem Ton.

And she thought of herself, 39.3

Und sie dachte bei sich:

"I wish the creatures wouldn't be so easily offended!" 39.4

"Ich wünschte, die Kreaturen wären nicht so leicht zu kränken!"

40.1 "You'll get used to it in time,"

"Du wirst dich mit der Zeit daran gewöhnen,"

40.2 said the Caterpillar; and it put the hookah into its mouth and began smoking again.

sagte die Raupe, steckte sich die Wasserpfeife in den Mund und begann wieder zu rauchen.

41.1 This time Alice waited patiently until it chose to speak again.

Diesmal wartete Alice geduldig, bis sie sich entschloss, wieder zu sprechen.

41.2 In a minute or two the Caterpillar took the hookah out of its mouth and yawned once or twice,

Nach ein oder zwei Minuten nahm die Raupe die Wasserpfeife aus dem Mund,

41.3 and shook itself.

gähnte ein oder zwei Mal und schüttelte sich.

41.4 Then it got down off the mushroom, and crawled away in the grass, merely remarking as it went:

Dann stieg sie von dem Pilz herunter und kroch im Gras davon, wobei sie lediglich bemerkte:

41.5 "One side will make you grow taller,

"Auf der einen Seite wirst du größer,

41.6 and the other side will make you grow shorter."

auf der anderen Seite kleiner."

42.1 "One side of what? The other side of what?"

"Eine Seite von was? Die andere Seite von was?"

thought Alice to herself. 42.2

dachte Alice bei sich.

"Of the mushroom," 43.1

"Von dem Pilz,"

said the Caterpillar, just as if she had asked it aloud; 43.2
and in another moment it was out of sight.

sagte die Raupe, als hätte sie es laut gefragt, und im
nächsten Augenblick war sie außer Sichtweite.

Alice remained looking thoughtfully at the 44.1
mushroom for a minute,

Alice betrachtete den Pilz eine Minute lang nachdenklich
und versuchte herauszufinden,

trying to make out which were the two sides of it; 44.2

welches die beiden Seiten des Pilzes waren;

and as it was perfectly round, 44.3

und da er vollkommen rund war,

she found this a very difficult question. 44.4

fand sie diese Frage sehr schwierig.

However, at last she stretched her arms round it as far 44.5
as they would go, and broke off a bit of the edge with
each hand.

Doch schließlich streckte sie ihre Arme so weit wie möglich
aus und brach mit jeder Hand ein Stück des Randes ab.

"And now which is which?" 45.1

"Und was ist nun was?"

45.2 **she said to herself,**

sagte sie zu sich selbst und knabberte ein wenig an dem rechten Stück,

45.3 **and nibbled a little of the right-hand bit to try the effect:**

um die Wirkung zu testen:

45.4 **the next moment she felt a violent blow underneath her chin:**

Im nächsten Moment spürte sie einen heftigen Schlag unter ihrem Kinn:

45.5 **it had struck her foot!**

Es hatte ihren Fuß getroffen!

46.1 **She was a good deal frightened by this very sudden change, but she felt that there was no time to be lost, as she was shrinking rapidly; so she set to work at once to eat some of the other bit.**

Diese plötzliche Veränderung erschreckte sie sehr, aber sie spürte, dass es keine Zeit zu verlieren gab, da sie schnell schrumpfte, und machte sich sofort daran, etwas von dem anderen Gebiss zu essen.

46.2 **Her chin was pressed so closely against her foot, that there was hardly room to open her mouth; but she did it at last, and managed to swallow a morsel of the lefthand bit.**

Ihr Kinn wurde so eng an den Fuß gepresst, dass sie kaum den Mund öffnen konnte, aber sie schaffte es schließlich und schluckte einen Bissen des linken Gebisses.

"Come, my head's free at last!"

48.1

"Komm, mein Kopf ist endlich frei!"

said Alice in a tone of delight, which changed into
alarm in another moment, when she found that her
shoulders were nowhere to be found:

48.2

sagte Alice in einem Ton der Freude, der sich im nächsten
Moment in einen Schreck verwandelte, als sie feststellte,
dass ihre Schultern nirgends zu finden waren:

all she could see, when she looked down, was an
immense length of neck, which seemed to rise like
a stalk out of a sea of green leaves that lay far below
her.

48.3

Alles, was sie sehen konnte, wenn sie nach unten blickte,
war ein riesiger Hals, der wie ein Halm aus einem Meer von
grünen Blättern zu ragen schien, das weit unter ihr lag.

"What can all that green stuff be?" said Alice.

49.1

"Was kann all das grüne Zeug sein?" fragte Alice.

"And where have my shoulders got to?

49.2

"Und wo sind meine Schultern geblieben?

And oh, my poor hands, how is it I can't see you?"

49.3

Und oh, meine armen Hände, wie kommt es, dass ich dich
nicht sehen kann?"

She was moving them about as she spoke, but no
result seemed to follow, except a little shaking among
the distant green leaves.

49.4

Sie bewegte sie, während sie sprach, aber es schien kein
Ergebnis zu geben, außer einem kleinen Zittern zwischen
den fernen grünen Blättern.

50.1 As there seemed to be no chance of getting her hands up to her head, she tried to get her head down to them, and was delighted to find that her neck would bend about easily in any direction, like a serpent.

Da es keine Möglichkeit gab, die Hände zum Kopf zu heben, versuchte sie, den Kopf nach unten zu bringen, und stellte erfreut fest, dass sich ihr Hals wie eine Schlange leicht in jede Richtung biegen ließ.

50.2 She had just succeeded in curving it down into a graceful zigzag, and was going to dive in among the leaves, which she found to be nothing but the tops of the trees under which she had been wandering, when a sharp hiss made her draw back in a hurry:

Gerade war es ihr gelungen, ihn zu einem anmutigen Zickzack zu biegen, und sie wollte zwischen den Blättern hindurchtauchen, die, wie sie feststellte, nichts anderes waren als die Wipfel der Bäume, unter denen sie umhergewandert war, als ein scharfes Zischen sie eilig zurückweichen ließ:

50.3 a large pigeon had flown into her face, and was beating her violently with its wings.

eine große Taube war ihr ins Gesicht geflogen und schlug heftig mit den Flügeln.

51.1 "Serpent!" screamed the Pigeon.

"Schlange!" schrie die Taube.

52.1 "I'm not a serpent!" said Alice indignantly.

"Ich bin keine Schlange," sagte Alice entrüstet.

52.2 "Let me alone!"

"Lasst mich in Ruhe!"

"Serpent, I say again!"   53.1
"Schlange, ich wiederhole!"

repeated the Pigeon, but in a more subdued tone, and   53.2
added with a kind of sob,
wiederholte die Taube, aber in einem gedämpften Ton, und
fügte mit einer Art Schluchzen hinzu:

"I've tried every way, and nothing seems to suit   53.3
them!"
"Ich habe alles versucht, und nichts scheint ihnen zu
passen!"

"I haven't the least idea what you're talking about,"   54.1
"Ich habe nicht die geringste Ahnung, wovon du redest,"

said Alice.   54.2
sagte Alice.

"I've tried the roots of trees, and I've tried banks, and   55.1
I've tried hedges,"
"Ich habe es mit den Wurzeln der Bäume versucht, und ich
habe es mit Banken und Hecken versucht,"

the Pigeon went on, without attending to her;   55.2
fuhr die Taube fort, ohne sich um sie zu kümmern,

"but those serpents! There's no pleasing them!"   55.3
"aber diese Schlangen! Man kann sie nicht besänftigen!"

Alice was more and more puzzled, but she thought   56.1
there was no use in saying anything more till the
Pigeon had finished.
Alice war immer verwirrter, aber sie hielt es für sinnlos,
noch etwas zu sagen, bis die Taube geendet hatte.

57.1 "As if it wasn't trouble enough hatching the eggs,"
"Als ob es nicht schon schwierig genug wäre, die Eier auszubrüten,"

57.2 said the Pigeon;
sagte die Taube,

57.3 "but I must be on the look-out for serpents night and day!
"aber ich muss auch Tag und Nacht nach Schlangen Ausschau halten!

57.4 Why, I haven't had a wink of sleep these three weeks!"
Ich habe seit drei Wochen kein Auge zugetan!"

58.1 "I'm very sorry you've been annoyed,"
"Es tut mir sehr leid, dass du dich geärgert hast,"

58.2 said Alice, who was beginning to see its meaning.
sagte Alice, die langsam den Sinn des Ganzen erkannte.

59.1 "And just as I'd taken the highest tree in the wood,"
"Und gerade als ich den höchsten Baum des Waldes erklommen hatte,"

59.2 continued the Pigeon, raising its voice to a shriek,
fuhr die Taube fort und erhob ihre Stimme zu einem Schrei,

59.3 "and just as I was thinking I should be free of them at last, they must needs come wriggling down from the sky!
"und gerade als ich dachte, dass ich endlich von ihnen befreit sein würde, müssen sie vom Himmel heruntergekrochen kommen!

Ugh, Serpent!"   59.4
Pfui, Schlange!"

"But I'm not a serpent, I tell you!" said Alice.   60.1
"Aber ich bin doch keine Schlange!" sagte Alice.

"I'm a — I'm a — "   60.2
"Ich bin eine — ich bin eine — "

"Well! What are you?" said the Pigeon.   61.1
"Nun! Was bist du?" sagte die Taube.

"I can see you're trying to invent something!"   61.2
"Ich sehe, dass du versuchst, etwas zu erfinden!"

"I — I'm a little girl,"   62.1
"Ich bin ein kleines Mädchen,"

said Alice, rather doubtfully, as she remembered the   62.2
number of changes she had gone through that day.
sagte Alice etwas unsicher, als sie sich an die vielen
Veränderungen erinnerte, die sie an diesem Tag
durchgemacht hatte.

"A likely story indeed!"   63.1
"Eine wahrhaft wahrscheinliche Geschichte,"

said the Pigeon in a tone of the deepest contempt.   63.2
sagte die Taube in einem Ton der tiefsten Verachtung.

"I've seen a good many little girls in my time,   63.3
"Ich habe in meinem Leben schon viele kleine Mädchen
gesehen,

63.4 but never one with such a neck as that! No, no!
aber noch nie eines mit einem solchen Hals! Nein, nein!

63.5 You're a serpent; and there's no use denying it.
Du bist eine Schlange, und es hat keinen Sinn, es zu
leugnen.

63.6 I suppose you'll be telling me next that you never
tasted an egg!"
Ich nehme an, du wirst mir als nächstes erzählen, dass du
noch nie ein Ei gekostet hast!"

64.1 "I have tasted eggs, certainly,"
"Natürlich habe ich Eier gekostet,"

64.2 said Alice, who was a very truthful child;
sagte Alice, die ein sehr ehrliches Kind war,

64.3 "but little girls eat eggs quite as much as serpents do,
"aber kleine Mädchen essen Eier genauso gerne wie
Schlangen,

64.4 you know."
weißt du."

65.1 "I don't believe it," said the Pigeon;
"Ich glaube es nicht," sagte die Taube,

65.2 "but if they do, why then they're a kind of serpent,
that's all I can say."
"aber wenn sie es tun, dann sind sie eine Art Schlange, das
ist alles, was ich sagen kann."

This was such a new idea to Alice, that she was quite silent for a minute or two, which gave the Pigeon the opportunity of adding: 66.1

Das war eine so neue Idee für Alice, dass sie für ein oder zwei Minuten ganz still war, was der Taube die Gelegenheit gab, hinzuzufügen:

"You're looking for eggs, I know that well enough; 66.2

"Du suchst Eier, das weiß ich sehr gut;

and what does it matter to me whether you're a little girl or a serpent?" 66.3

und was macht es für mich aus, ob du ein kleines Mädchen oder eine Schlange bist?"

"It matters a good deal to me," said Alice hastily; 67.1

"Es ist mir sehr wichtig," sagte Alice hastig,

but I'm not looking for eggs, as it happens; and if I was, I shouldn't want yours: 67.2

"aber ich suche keine Eier, und wenn ich welche bräuchte, würde ich deine nicht wollen:

I don't like them raw." 67.3

Ich mag sie nicht roh."

"Well, be off, then!" said the Pigeon in a sulky tone, 68.1

"Na, dann hau doch ab!" sagte die Taube mürrisch,

as it settled down again into its nest. 68.2

als sie sich wieder in ihr Nest zurückzog.

68.3 Alice crouched down among the trees as well as she could, for her neck kept getting entangled among the branches, and every now and then she had to stop and untwist it.

Alice kauerte so gut es ging zwischen den Bäumen, denn ihr Hals verhedderte sich immer wieder zwischen den Ästen, und immer wieder musste sie innehalten und ihn entwirren.

68.4 After a while she remembered that she still held the pieces of mushroom in her hands, and she set to work very carefully, nibbling first at one and then at the other, and growing sometimes taller and sometimes shorter, until she had succeeded in bringing herself down to her usual height.

Nach einer Weile erinnerte sie sich daran, dass sie immer noch die Pilzstücke in den Händen hielt, und sie machte sich ganz vorsichtig an die Arbeit, knabberte erst an dem einen und dann an dem anderen und wurde mal größer und mal kleiner, bis sie es geschafft hatte, sich auf ihre übliche Größe zu bringen.

69.1 It was so long since she had been anything near the right size, that it felt quite strange at first;

Es war so lange her, dass sie auch nur annähernd die richtige Größe gehabt hatte, dass es sich zunächst ziemlich seltsam anfühlte;

69.2 but she got used to it in a few minutes, and began talking to herself, as usual.

aber nach ein paar Minuten hatte sie sich daran gewöhnt und begann wie üblich mit sich selbst zu reden.

69.3 "Come, there's half my plan done now!

"Komm, jetzt ist die Hälfte meines Plans fertig!

How puzzling all these changes are!   69.4
Wie rätselhaft all diese Veränderungen sind!

I'm never sure what I'm going to be,   69.5
Ich bin nie sicher,

from one minute to another!   69.6
was ich von einer Minute zur anderen sein werde!

However, I've got back to my right size: 69.7
Aber jetzt habe ich wieder meine richtige Größe:

the next thing is, to get into that beautiful garden -   69.8
jetzt muss ich nur noch in diesen schönen Garten
kommen -

how is that to be done, I wonder?"   69.9
wie das wohl gehen soll?"

As she said this, she came suddenly upon an open   69.10
place, with a little house in it about four feet high.
Während sie dies sagte, kam sie plötzlich auf einen offenen
Platz, auf dem ein kleines Haus stand, das etwa vier Fuß
hoch war.

"Whoever lives there," thought Alice,   69.11
"Wer auch immer dort wohnt," dachte Alice,

"it'll never do to come upon them this size: 69.12
"es ist nicht gut, wenn ich sie in dieser Größe antreffe:

why, I should frighten them out of their wits!"   69.13
ich würde sie zu Tode erschrecken!"

So she began nibbling at the righthand bit again,   69.14
Also begann sie wieder an dem rechten Gebiss zu knabbern
und wagte sich erst in die Nähe des Hauses,

69.15 **and did not venture to go near the house till she had brought herself down to nine inches high.**

als sie sich auf eine Höhe von neun Zoll gebracht hatte.

CHAPTER VI. Pig and Pepper

KAPITEL VI. Schwein und Paprika

1.1 For a minute or two she stood looking at the house, and wondering what to do next, when suddenly a footman in livery came running out of the wood — (she considered him to be a footman because he was in livery: otherwise, judging by his face only, she would have called him a fish) — and rapped loudly at the door with his knuckles.

Ein oder zwei Minuten lang stand sie vor dem Haus und überlegte, was sie als Nächstes tun sollte, als plötzlich ein Lakai in Livree aus dem Wald kam (sie hielt ihn für einen Lakai, weil er eine Livree trug, sonst hätte sie ihn nach seinem Gesicht zu urteilen für einen Fisch gehalten) und laut mit den Fingerknöcheln an die Tür klopfte.

1.2 It was opened by another footman in livery, with a round face, and large eyes like a frog;

Sie wurde von einem anderen Lakaien in Livree geöffnet, der ein rundes Gesicht und große Augen wie ein Frosch hatte;

1.3 and both footmen, Alice noticed, had powdered hair that curled all over their heads.

und beide Lakaien, so bemerkte Alice, hatten gepudertes Haar, das sich über den ganzen Kopf kräuselte.

115

She felt very curious to know what it was all about, and crept a little way out of the wood to listen. 1.4

Sie war sehr neugierig zu erfahren, worum es ging, und schlich sich ein Stück aus dem Wald heraus, um zu lauschen.

The Fish-Footman began by producing from under his arm a great letter, nearly as large as himself, and this he handed over to the other, saying, in a solemn tone: 2.1

Der Fish-Footman begann damit, dass er unter seinem Arm einen großen Brief hervorholte, der fast so groß war wie er selbst, und diesen übergab er dem anderen mit den feierlichen Worten:

"For the Duchess. 2.2

"Für die Herzogin.

An invitation from the Queen to play croquet." 2.3

Eine Einladung der Königin zum Krocketspiel."

The Frog-Footman repeated, in the same solemn tone, only changing the order of the words a little: 2.4

Der Froschfussmann wiederholte in demselben feierlichen Ton, wobei er nur die Reihenfolge der Worte ein wenig änderte:

"From the Queen. 2.5

"Von der Königin.

An invitation for the Duchess to play croquet." 2.6

Eine Einladung für die Herzogin, Krocket zu spielen."

Then they both bowed low, 3.1

Dann verbeugten sich beide tief,

3.2 and their curls got entangled together.

und ihre Locken verhedderten sich.

4.1 Alice laughed so much at this, that she had to run back into the wood for fear of their hearing her;

Alice lachte darüber so sehr, dass sie in den Wald zurücklaufen musste, weil sie fürchtete, sie könnten sie hören;

4.2 and when she next peeped out the Fish-Footman was gone, and the other was sitting on the ground near the door, staring stupidly up into the sky.

und als sie das nächste Mal hinausspähte, war der Fischfußmann verschwunden, und der andere saß auf dem Boden neben der Tür und starrte dumm in den Himmel.

5.1 Alice went timidly up to the door, and knocked.

Alice ging zaghaft zur Tür und klopfte.

6.1 "There's no sort of use in knocking," said the Footman,

"Es hat keinen Sinn zu klopfen," sagte der Lakai,

6.2 "and that for two reasons.

"und zwar aus zwei Gründen.

6.3 First, because I'm on the same side of the door as you are; secondly, because they're making such a noise inside, no one could possibly hear you."

Erstens, weil ich auf der gleichen Seite der Tür stehe wie Sie, und zweitens, weil sie drinnen einen solchen Lärm machen, dass man Sie unmöglich hören kann."

And certainly there was a most extraordinary noise
going on within -

6.4

Und tatsächlich herrschte drinnen ein ganz
außergewöhnlicher Lärm -

a constant howling and sneezing, and every now
and then a great crash, as if a dish or kettle had been
broken to pieces.

6.5

ein ständiges Heulen und Niesen und hin und wieder ein
großes Krachen, als ob eine Schüssel oder ein Kessel in
Stücke zerbrochen wäre.

"Please, then," said Alice, "how am I to get in?"

7.1

"Bitte," sagte Alice, "wie komme ich dann rein?"

"There might be some sense in your knocking,"

8.1

"Es hätte vielleicht einen Sinn, wenn Sie klopfen würden,"

the Footman went on without attending to her,

8.2

fuhr der Lakai fort, ohne sie zu beachten,

"if we had the door between us.

8.3

"wenn wir die Tür zwischen uns hätten.

For instance, if you were inside, you might knock,
and I could let you out, you know."

8.4

Wenn du zum Beispiel drinnen wärst, könntest du klopfen,
und ich könnte dich hinauslassen, weißt du."

He was looking up into the sky all the time he was
speaking, and this Alice thought decidedly uncivil.

8.5

Während er sprach, blickte er die ganze Zeit in den
Himmel, und das fand Alice ausgesprochen unhöflich.

"But perhaps he can't help it,"

8.6

"Aber vielleicht kann er gar nicht anders,"

8.7 she said to herself;
sagte sie zu sich selbst,

8.8 "his eyes are so very nearly at the top of his head.
"seine Augen sind ja fast auf dem Kopf.

8.9 But at any rate he might answer questions.
Auf jeden Fall könnte er Fragen beantworten.

8.10 — How am I to get in?" she repeated, aloud.
Wie komme ich rein?" wiederholte sie laut.

9.1 "I shall sit here," the Footman remarked,
"Ich werde hier sitzen," sagte der Lakai,

9.2 "till tomorrow — "
"bis morgen — "

10.1 At this moment the door of the house opened, and
a large plate came skimming out, straight at the
Footman's head: it just grazed his nose, and broke to
pieces against one of the trees behind him.
In diesem Augenblick öffnete sich die Tür des Hauses,
und ein großer Teller flog heraus, direkt auf den Kopf des
Lakaien zu, streifte seine Nase und zerschellte an einem der
Bäume hinter ihm.

11.1 " — or next day, maybe,"
"oder vielleicht am nächsten Tag,"

11.2 the Footman continued in the same tone,
fuhr der Lakai in demselben Ton fort,

11.3 exactly as if nothing had happened.
als ob nichts geschehen wäre.

"How am I to get in?"   12.1
"Wie komme ich da rein?"

asked Alice again, in a louder tone.   12.2
fragte Alice erneut und mit lauterem Ton.

"Are you to get in at all?" said the Footman.   13.1
"Kommst du überhaupt rein?" fragte der Lakai.

"That's the first question, you know."   13.2
"Das ist die erste Frage, wissen Sie."

It was, no doubt: only Alice did not like to be told so.   14.1
Zweifellos war es so, nur wollte Alice das nicht hören.

"It's really dreadful," she muttered to herself,   14.2
"Es ist wirklich furchtbar," murmelte sie vor sich hin,

"the way all the creatures argue.   14.3
"wie sich alle Kreaturen streiten.

It's enough to drive one crazy!"   14.4
Das ist zum Verrücktwerden!"

The Footman seemed to think this a good   15.1
opportunity for repeating his remark,
Der Lakai schien dies für eine gute Gelegenheit zu halten,

with variations.   15.2
seine Bemerkung in abgewandelter Form zu wiederholen.

"I shall sit here," he said, "on and off,   15.3
"Ich werde hier sitzen," sagte er, "immer wieder,

15.4 for days and days."
tagelang."

16.1 "But what am I to do?" said Alice.
"Aber was soll ich tun?" fragte Alice.

17.1 "Anything you like," said the Footman, and began whistling.
"Alles, was Sie wollen," sagte der Lakai und begann zu pfeifen.

18.1 "Oh, there's no use in talking to him,"
"Oh, es hat keinen Sinn, mit ihm zu reden,"

18.2 said Alice desperately: "he's perfectly idiotic!"
sagte Alice verzweifelt: "Er ist vollkommen idiotisch!"

18.3 And she opened the door and went in.
Und sie öffnete die Tür und ging hinein.

19.1 The door led right into a large kitchen,
Die Tür führte direkt in eine große Küche,

19.2 which was full of smoke from one end to the other:
die von einem Ende bis zum anderen voller Rauch war:

19.3 the Duchess was sitting on a three-legged stool in the middle, nursing a baby;
Die Herzogin saß auf einem dreibeinigen Schemel in der Mitte und stillte ein Baby;

19.4 the cook was leaning over the fire,
die Köchin beugte sich über das Feuer und rührte in einem großen Kessel,

stirring a large cauldron which seemed to be full of soup. 19.5
der mit Suppe gefüllt zu sein schien.

"There's certainly too much pepper in that soup!" 20.1
"In dieser Suppe ist eindeutig zu viel Pfeffer!"

Alice said to herself, as well as she could for sneezing. 20.2
sagte Alice zu sich selbst, so gut sie es konnte, weil sie niesen musste.

There was certainly too much of it in the air. 21.1
Es lag einfach zu viel davon in der Luft.

Even the Duchess sneezed occasionally; and as for the baby, 21.2
Sogar die Herzogin nieste gelegentlich,

it was sneezing and howling alternately without a moment's pause. 21.3
und das Baby nieste und heulte abwechselnd ohne Unterbrechung.

The only things in the kitchen that did not sneeze, were the cook, and a large cat which was sitting on the hearth and grinning from ear to ear. 21.4
Die einzigen, die in der Küche nicht niesen mussten, waren die Köchin und eine große Katze, die auf dem Herd saß und von Ohr zu Ohr grinste.

"Please would you tell me," 22.1
"Würden Sie mir bitte sagen,"

22.2 said Alice, a little timidly, for she was not quite sure whether it was good manners for her to speak first,

sagte Alice ein wenig zaghaft, denn sie war sich nicht ganz sicher, ob es zum guten Ton gehörte, zuerst zu sprechen,

22.3 "why your cat grins like that?"

"warum Ihre Katze so grinst?"

23.1 "It's a Cheshire cat," said the Duchess,

"Es ist eine Grinsekatze," sagte die Herzogin,

23.2 "and that's why. Pig!"

"und das ist der Grund. Schwein!"

24.1 She said the last word with such sudden violence that Alice quite jumped;

Das letzte Wort sagte sie mit so plötzlicher Heftigkeit, dass Alice zusammenzuckte;

24.2 but she saw in another moment that it was addressed to the baby, and not to her, so she took courage, and went on again: — .

aber in einem anderen Augenblick sah sie, dass es an das Baby und nicht an sie gerichtet war, und so fasste sie Mut und fuhr fort.

25.1 "I didn't know that Cheshire cats always grinned;

"Ich wusste nicht, dass Grinsekatzen immer grinsen;

25.2 in fact, I didn't know that cats could grin."

ich wusste sogar nicht, dass Katzen grinsen können."

"They all can," said the Duchess; "and most of 'em do."

26.1

"Das können sie alle," sagte die Herzogin, "und die meisten von ihnen tun es auch."

"I don't know of any that do,"

27.1

"Ich kenne keine, die das tun,"

Alice said very politely,

27.2

sagte Alice sehr höflich und freute sich,

feeling quite pleased to have got into a conversation.

27.3

dass sie in ein Gespräch kam.

"You don't know much," said the Duchess;

28.1

"Sie wissen nicht viel," sagte die Herzogin,

"and that's a fact."

28.2

"und das ist eine Tatsache."

Alice did not at all like the tone of this remark, and thought it would be as well to introduce some other subject of conversation.

29.1

Alice gefiel der Ton dieser Bemerkung ganz und gar nicht, und sie dachte, es wäre besser, ein anderes Gesprächsthema zu finden.

While she was trying to fix on one, the cook took the cauldron of soup off the fire, and at once set to work throwing everything within her reach at the Duchess and the baby -

29.2

Während sie versuchte, ein solches zu finden, nahm die Köchin den Kessel mit der Suppe vom Feuer und machte sich sofort daran, alles, was in ihrer Reichweite lag, auf die Herzogin und das Baby zu werfen -

29.3 the fire-irons came first; then followed a shower of saucepans, plates, and dishes.

zuerst die Feuereisen, dann ein Regen von Töpfen, Tellern und Schalen.

29.4 The Duchess took no notice of them even when they hit her; and the baby was howling so much already, that it was quite impossible to say whether the blows hurt it or not.

Die Herzogin beachtete sie nicht, auch wenn sie sie trafen, und das Baby heulte schon so sehr, dass man nicht sagen konnte, ob die Schläge ihm wehtaten oder nicht.

30.1 "Oh, please mind what you're doing!"

"Oh, bitte pass auf, was du tust!"

30.2 cried Alice, jumping up and down in an agony of terror.

rief Alice und sprang in einem Anfall von Angst auf und ab.

30.3 "Oh, there goes his precious nose!"

"Oh, da fliegt seine kostbare Nase!"

30.4 as an unusually large saucepan flew close by it, and very nearly carried it off.

als ein ungewöhnlich großer Kochtopf dicht an ihr vorbeifliegt und sie beinahe mitreißt.

31.1 "If everybody minded their own business,"

"Wenn sich jeder um seinen eigenen Kram kümmern würde,"

31.2 the Duchess said in a hoarse growl,

sagte die Herzogin mit heiserem Knurren,

"the world would go round a deal faster than it does."   31.3

"würde sich die Welt viel schneller drehen, als sie es tut."

"Which would not be an advantage,"   32.1

"Das wäre nicht von Vorteil,"

said Alice, who felt very glad to get an opportunity of   32.2
showing off a little of her knowledge.

sagte Alice, die sich sehr über die Gelegenheit freute, ein
wenig von ihrem Wissen zeigen zu können.

"Just think of what work it would make with the day   32.3
and night!

"Denken Sie nur daran, was das für eine Arbeit mit dem
Tag und der Nacht machen würde!

You see the earth takes twenty-four hours to turn   32.4
round on its axis — "

Die Erde braucht vierundzwanzig Stunden, um sich um die
eigene Achse zu drehen ..."

"Talking of axes," said the Duchess,   33.1

"Apropos Axt," sagte die Herzogin,

"chop off her head!"   33.2

"schlagt ihr den Kopf ab!"

Alice glanced rather anxiously at the cook, to see if   34.1
she meant to take the hint; but the cook was busily
stirring the soup, and seemed not to be listening, so
she went on again:

Alice warf der Köchin einen besorgten Blick zu, um zu
sehen, ob sie die Andeutung ernst nehmen würde, aber
die Köchin rührte eifrig in der Suppe und schien nicht
zuzuhören, also fuhr sie fort:

34.2 "Twenty-four hours, I think; or is it twelve?
"Vierundzwanzig Stunden, glaube ich; oder sind es zwölf?

34.3 I — "
I — "

35.1 "Oh, don't bother me," said the Duchess;
"Ach, stören Sie mich nicht," sagte die Herzogin,

35.2 "I never could abide figures!"
"ich konnte Figuren nie ausstehen!"

35.3 And with that she began nursing her child again, singing a sort of lullaby to it as she did so, and giving it a violent shake at the end of every line:
Und damit begann sie ihr Kind wieder zu stillen, sang ihm dabei eine Art Schlaflied und schüttelte es am Ende jeder Zeile kräftig:

"Speak roughly to your little boy,	"Sprich grob zu deinem kleinen Jungen,
And beat him when he sneezes:	Und schlagen Sie ihn, wenn er niest:
He only does it to annoy,	Er tut das nur, um zu ärgern,
Because he knows it teases."	Weil er weiß, dass es reizt."
CHORUS.	CHORUS.
(In which the cook and the baby joined):	(Wobei der Koch und das Baby mitmachen):

"Wow! wow! wow!"   "Wow, wow, wow!"   38.1

While the Duchess sang the second verse of the song,   39.1
she kept tossing the baby violently up and down,
and the poor little thing howled so, that Alice could
hardly hear the words: — .

Während die Herzogin die zweite Strophe des Liedes sang,
warf sie das Baby immer wieder heftig auf und ab, und das
arme kleine Ding heulte so sehr, dass Alice die Worte kaum
verstehen konnte.

"I speak severely to my boy,   "Ich spreche streng mit
                                    meinem Jungen,

I beat him when he sneezes;   Ich schlage ihn, wenn er
                                    niest;

For he can thoroughly enjoy   Denn er kann durch und
                                    durch genießen

The pepper when he   Der Pfeffer, wann er
pleases!"   will!"

CHORUS.   41.1
CHORUS.

"Wow! wow! wow!"   42.1
"Wow, wow, wow!"

"Here! you may nurse it a bit, if you like!"   43.1
"Hier, du kannst es ein wenig stillen, wenn du willst,"

the Duchess said to Alice, flinging the baby at her as   43.2
she spoke.
sagte die Herzogin zu Alice und warf ihr das Baby zu.

43.3 "I must go and get ready to play croquet with the Queen,"

"Ich muss gehen und mich für das Krocketspiel mit der Königin fertig machen,"

43.4 and she hurried out of the room.

und sie verließ eilig das Zimmer.

43.5 The cook threw a frying-pan after her as she went out,

Die Köchin warf ihr eine Bratpfanne hinterher,

43.6 but it just missed her.

aber sie verfehlte sie knapp.

44.1 Alice caught the baby with some difficulty, as it was a queer-shaped little creature, and held out its arms and legs in all directions,

Alice hatte einige Mühe, das Baby zu fangen, denn es war ein seltsam geformtes kleines Wesen und streckte seine Arme und Beine in alle Richtungen aus,

44.2 "just like a star-fish," thought Alice.

"wie ein Sternenfisch," dachte Alice.

44.3 The poor little thing was snorting like a steam-engine when she caught it, and kept doubling itself up and straightening itself out again, so that altogether, for the first minute or two, it was as much as she could do to hold it.

Das arme kleine Ding schnaubte wie eine Dampfmaschine, als sie es auffing, und es drehte sich immer wieder zusammen und richtete sich wieder auf, so dass sie es in den ersten ein oder zwei Minuten nur mit Mühe halten konnte.

As soon as she had made out the proper way of nursing it, (which was to twist it up into a sort of knot, and then keep tight hold of its right ear and left foot, so as to prevent its undoing itself,) she carried it out into the open air.

45.1

Sobald sie herausgefunden hatte, wie sie es am besten stillen konnte, nämlich indem sie es zu einer Art Knoten zusammenzog und dann das rechte Ohr und den linken Fuß festhielt, damit es sich nicht selbst auflöste, trug sie es ins Freie.

"If I don't take this child away with me," thought Alice,

45.2

"Wenn ich dieses Kind nicht mitnehme," dachte Alice,

"they're sure to kill it in a day or two:

45.3

"werden sie es sicher in ein oder zwei Tagen umbringen:

wouldn't it be murder to leave it behind?"

45.4

wäre es nicht Mord, es zurückzulassen?"

She said the last words out loud,

45.5

Sie sprach die letzten Worte laut aus,

and the little thing grunted in reply (it had left off sneezing by this time).

45.6

und das kleine Ding grunzte als Antwort (es hatte inzwischen aufgehört zu niesen).

"Don't grunt," said Alice;

45.7

"Grunz nicht," sagte Alice,

"that's not at all a proper way of expressing yourself."

45.8

"das ist keine angemessene Art, sich auszudrücken."

46.1 **The baby grunted again, and Alice looked very anxiously into its face to see what was the matter with it.**

Das Baby grunzte wieder, und Alice schaute ihm ängstlich ins Gesicht, um zu sehen, was mit ihm los war.

46.2 **There could be no doubt that it had a very turn-up nose,**

Zweifellos hatte es eine sehr hochgezogene Nase,

46.3 **much more like a snout than a real nose;**

die eher einer Schnauze als einer echten Nase glich;

46.4 **also its eyes were getting extremely small for a baby:**

auch seine Augen waren für ein Baby sehr klein geworden:

46.5 **altogether Alice did not like the look of the thing at all.**

Insgesamt gefiel Alice das Aussehen des Dings überhaupt nicht.

46.6 **"But perhaps it was only sobbing,"**

"Aber vielleicht hat es nur geschluchzt,"

46.7 **she thought, and looked into its eyes again, to see if there were any tears.**

dachte sie und schaute noch einmal in seine Augen, um zu sehen, ob es Tränen gab.

47.1 **No, there were no tears.**

Nein, es gab keine Tränen.

47.2 **"If you're going to turn into a pig, my dear,"**

"Wenn du dich in ein Schwein verwandeln willst, meine Liebe," said Alice, seriously,   47.3

sagte Alice ernst,

"I'll have nothing more to do with you. Mind now!"   47.4

"dann will ich nichts mehr mit dir zu tun haben. Pass mal
auf!"

The poor little thing sobbed again (or grunted, it was   47.5
impossible to say which), and they went on for some
while in silence.

Das arme kleine Ding schluchzte wieder (oder grunzte, es
war unmöglich zu sagen, was), und sie gingen eine Weile
schweigend weiter.

Alice was just beginning to think to herself: 48.1

Alice überlegte gerade:

"Now,   48.2

"Was soll ich mit dieser Kreatur machen,

what am I to do with this creature when I get it   48.3
home?"

wenn ich sie nach Hause bringe?"

when it grunted again, so violently, that she looked   48.4
down into its face in some alarm.

als es erneut grunzte, so heftig, dass sie erschrocken in sein
Gesicht blickte.

This time there could be no mistake about it: 48.5

Diesmal konnte sie sich nicht irren:

it was neither more nor less than a pig, and she   48.6
felt that it would be quite absurd for her to carry it
further.

Es war weder mehr noch weniger als ein Schwein, und sie
hielt es für völlig absurd, es weiter zu tragen.

49.1 So she set the little creature down,
So setzte sie das kleine Wesen ab und war erleichtert,

49.2 and felt quite relieved to see it trot away quietly into the wood.
als es leise in den Wald trottete.

49.3 "If it had grown up," she said to herself,
"Wenn es groß geworden wäre," sagte sie zu sich selbst,

49.4 "it would have made a dreadfully ugly child: but it makes rather a handsome pig, I think."
"wäre es ein furchtbar hässliches Kind geworden, aber es ist ein hübsches Schwein, finde ich."

49.5 And she began thinking over other children she knew, who might do very well as pigs, and was just saying to herself:
Und sie dachte an andere Kinder, die sie kannte und die sich sehr gut als Schweine eignen würden, und sagte gerade zu sich selbst:

49.6 "if one only knew the right way to change them — "
"Wenn man nur wüsste, wie man sie umwandeln könnte — ,"

49.7 when she was a little startled by seeing the Cheshire Cat sitting on a bough of a tree a few yards off.
als sie ein wenig erschrak, als sie die Grinsekatze ein paar Meter entfernt auf einem Baumzweig sitzen sah.

50.1 The Cat only grinned when it saw Alice.
Die Katze grinste nur, als sie Alice sah.

It looked good-natured, she thought: still it had very long claws and a great many teeth, so she felt that it ought to be treated with respect. 50.2

Sie sah gutmütig aus, dachte sie, aber sie hatte sehr lange Krallen und viele Zähne, so dass sie fand, dass man sie mit Respekt behandeln sollte.

"Cheshire Puss," 51.1

"Cheshire Puss,"

she began, rather timidly, as she did not at all know whether it would like the name: however, it only grinned a little wider. 51.2

begann sie etwas zaghaft, da sie nicht wusste, ob ihm der Name gefallen würde, aber er grinste nur noch breiter.

"Come, it's pleased so far," 51.3

"Komm, es ist so weit zufrieden,"

thought Alice, and she went on. 51.4

dachte Alice und fuhr fort.

"Would you tell me, please, which way I ought to go from here?" 51.5

"Würden Sie mir bitte sagen, in welche Richtung ich von hier aus gehen soll?"

"That depends a good deal on where you want to get to," 52.1

"Das hängt sehr davon ab, wo Sie hinwollen,"

said the Cat. 52.2

sagte die Katze.

53.1 "I don't much care where — " said Alice.
"Es ist mir ziemlich egal, wo," sagte Alice.

54.1 "Then it doesn't matter which way you go," said the Cat.
"Dann ist es egal, welchen Weg du gehst," sagte die Katze.

55.1 " — so long as I get somewhere,"
"Hauptsache, ich komme weiter,"

55.2 Alice added as an explanation.
fügte Alice als Erklärung hinzu.

56.1 "Oh, you're sure to do that," said the Cat,
"Oh, das wirst du sicher tun," sagte die Katze,

56.2 "if you only walk long enough."
"wenn du nur lange genug läufst."

57.1 Alice felt that this could not be denied, so she tried another question.
Alice spürte, dass dies nicht zu leugnen war, also versuchte sie es mit einer anderen Frage.

57.2 "What sort of people live about here?"
"Was für Leute leben hier in der Gegend?"

58.1 "In that direction,"
"In dieser Richtung,"

58.2 the Cat said, waving its right paw round,
sagte die Katze und winkte mit der rechten Pfote,

"lives a Hatter: and in that direction," 58.3
"lebt ein Hutmacher; und in dieser Richtung,"

waving the other paw, "lives a March Hare. 58.4
sie winkte mit der anderen Pfote, "lebt ein Märzhase.

Visit either you like: they're both mad." 58.5
Besucht einen von beiden, sie sind beide verrückt."

"But I don't want to go among mad people," Alice 59.1
remarked.
"Aber ich will nicht unter Verrückte gehen," bemerkte
Alice.

"Oh, you can't help that," said the Cat: 60.1
"Da kann man nichts machen," sagte die Katze:

"we're all mad here. I'm mad. 60.2
"wir sind hier alle verrückt. Ich bin verrückt.

You're mad." 60.3
Du bist verrückt."

"How do you know I'm mad?" said Alice. 61.1
"Woher weißt du, dass ich verrückt bin?" fragte Alice.

"You must be," said the Cat, 62.1
"Du musst es sein," sagte die Katze,

"or you wouldn't have come here." 62.2
"sonst wärst du nicht hergekommen."

Alice didn't think that proved it at all; however, she 63.1
went on:
Alice fand das überhaupt nicht bewiesen, fuhr aber fort:

63.2 "And how do you know that you're mad?"
"Und woher weißt du, dass du verrückt bist?"

64.1 "To begin with," said the Cat,
"Zunächst einmal," sagte die Katze,

64.2 "a dog's not mad. You grant that?"
"ist ein Hund nicht verrückt. Ist das klar?"

65.1 "I suppose so," said Alice.
"Ich denke schon," sagte Alice.

66.1 "Well, then," the Cat went on,
"Nun," fuhr die Katze fort,

66.2 "you see, a dog growls when it's angry, and wags its tail when it's pleased.
"ein Hund knurrt, wenn er wütend ist, und wedelt mit dem Schwanz, wenn er zufrieden ist.

66.3 Now I growl when I'm pleased, and wag my tail when I'm angry.
Ich aber knurre, wenn ich zufrieden bin, und wedle mit dem Schwanz, wenn ich wütend bin.

66.4 Therefore I'm mad."
Deshalb bin ich wütend."

67.1 "I call it purring, not growling," said Alice.
"Ich nenne es Schnurren, nicht Knurren," sagte Alice.

68.1 "Call it what you like," said the Cat.
"Nenn es, wie du willst," sagte die Katze.

"Do you play croquet with the Queen to- day?"   68.2
"Spielst du heute Krocket mit der Königin?"

"I should like it very much," said Alice,   69.1
"Ich würde sehr gerne kommen," sagte Alice,

"but I haven't been invited yet."   69.2
"aber ich bin noch nicht eingeladen worden."

"You'll see me there," said the Cat, and vanished.   70.1
"Du wirst mich dort sehen," sagte die Katze und
verschwand.

Alice was not much surprised at this, she was getting   71.1
so used to queer things happening.
Alice war darüber nicht sonderlich überrascht, denn sie
hatte sich daran gewöhnt, dass seltsame Dinge passierten.

While she was looking at the place where it had been,   71.2
it suddenly appeared again.
Während sie die Stelle betrachtete, an der es gewesen war,
tauchte es plötzlich wieder auf.

"By-the-bye, what became of the baby?" said the Cat.   72.1
"Übrigens, was ist aus dem Baby geworden?" fragte die
Katze.

"I'd nearly forgotten to ask."   72.2
"Ich hatte fast vergessen zu fragen."

"It turned into a pig," Alice quietly said,   73.1
"Es hat sich in ein Schwein verwandelt," sagte Alice leise,

73.2 just as if it had come back in a natural way.

als ob es auf natürliche Weise zurückgekommen wäre.

74.1 "I thought it would,"

"Das dachte ich mir schon,"

74.2 said the Cat, and vanished again.

sagte die Katze und verschwand wieder.

75.1 Alice waited a little, half expecting to see it again, but it did not appear, and after a minute or two she walked on in the direction in which the March Hare was said to live.

Alice wartete ein wenig, halb in der Erwartung, ihn wiederzusehen, aber er erschien nicht, und nach ein oder zwei Minuten ging sie weiter in die Richtung, in der der Märzhase leben sollte.

75.2 "I've seen hatters before,"

"Ich habe schon viele Hutmacher gesehen,"

75.3 she said to herself;

sagte sie zu sich selbst,

75.4 "the March Hare will be much the most interesting, and perhaps as this is May it won't be raving mad — at least not so mad as it was in March."

"der Märzhase wird am interessantesten sein, und da wir jetzt Mai haben, wird er vielleicht nicht so verrückt sein wie im März."

75.5 As she said this, she looked up, and there was the Cat again, sitting on a branch of a tree.

Während sie dies sagte, schaute sie auf, und da war wieder die Katze, die auf einem Baumzweig saß.

"Did you say pig, or fig?" said the Cat.　　　　　76.1
"Hast du Schwein oder Feige gesagt?" fragte die Katze.

"I said pig," replied Alice;　　　　　77.1
"Ich habe Schwein gesagt," antwortete Alice,

"and I wish you wouldn't keep appearing and　　　　　77.2
vanishing so suddenly:
"und ich wünschte, du würdest nicht immer so plötzlich
auftauchen und verschwinden:

you make one quite giddy."　　　　　77.3
du machst einen ganz schwindlig."

"All right,"　　　　　78.1
"In Ordnung,"

said the Cat; and this time it vanished quite slowly,　　　　　78.2
beginning with the end of the tail, and ending with
the grin, which remained some time after the rest of
it had gone.
sagte die Katze, und diesmal verschwand sie ganz langsam,
beginnend mit dem Ende des Schwanzes und endend mit
dem Grinsen, das noch einige Zeit blieb, nachdem der Rest
von ihr verschwunden war.

"Well! I've often seen a cat without a grin,"　　　　　79.1
"Nun! Ich habe schon oft eine Katze ohne Grinsen
gesehen,"

thought Alice; "but a grin without a cat!　　　　　79.2
dachte Alice, "aber ein Grinsen ohne Katze!

It's the most curious thing I ever saw in my life!"　　　　　79.3
Das ist das Seltsamste, was ich je in meinem Leben gesehen
habe!"

80.1 She had not gone much farther before she came in sight of the house of the March Hare:

Sie war noch nicht viel weiter gegangen, als sie das Haus des Märzhasen erblickte:

80.2 she thought it must be the right house, because the chimneys were shaped like ears and the roof was thatched with fur.

Sie dachte, es müsse das richtige Haus sein, weil die Schornsteine wie Ohren geformt waren und das Dach mit Fell bedeckt war.

80.3 It was so large a house, that she did not like to go nearer till she had nibbled some more of the lefthand bit of mushroom, and raised herself to about two feet high: even then she walked up towards it rather timidly, saying to herself

Es war ein so großes Haus, dass sie nicht näher gehen wollte, bevor sie nicht noch etwas von dem linken Pilzstück geknabbert und sich auf etwa zwei Fuß Höhe erhoben hatte; selbst dann ging sie eher zaghaft darauf zu und sagte zu sich selbst

80.4 "Suppose it should be raving mad after all! I almost wish I'd gone to see the Hatter instead!"

"Was, wenn es doch verrückt ist? Ich wünschte fast, ich hätte stattdessen den Hutmacher aufgesucht!"

CHAPTER VII. A Mad Tea-Party

KAPITEL VII. Eine verrückte Tee-Party

1.1 There was a table set out under a tree in front of the house,
Vor dem Haus war unter einem Baum ein Tisch gedeckt,

1.2 and the March Hare and the Hatter were having tea at it:
an dem der Märzhase und der Hutmacher Tee tranken:

1.3 a Dormouse was sitting between them, fast asleep, and the other two were using it as a cushion, resting their elbows on it, and talking over its head.
Zwischen ihnen saß eine Haselmaus, die fest schlief, und die beiden anderen benutzten sie als Kissen, stützten ihre Ellbogen auf sie und sprachen über ihren Kopf hinweg.

1.4 "Very uncomfortable for the Dormouse," thought Alice;
"Sehr unangenehm für die Haselmaus," dachte Alice,

1.5 "only, as it's asleep, I suppose it doesn't mind."
"aber da sie schläft, macht ihr das wohl nichts aus."

The table was a large one,   2.1
Der Tisch war groß,

but the three were all crowded together at one   2.2
corner of it:
aber die drei saßen dicht gedrängt in einer Ecke:

"No room! No room!"   2.3
"Kein Platz! Kein Platz!"

they cried out when they saw Alice coming.   2.4
riefen sie, als sie Alice kommen sahen.

"There's plenty of room!"   2.5
"Es ist genug Platz!"

said Alice indignantly, and she sat down in a large   2.6
arm-chair at one end of the table.
sagte Alice entrüstet und setzte sich in einen großen Sessel
an einem Ende des Tisches.

"Have some wine,"   3.1
"Nimm einen Schluck Wein,"

the March Hare said in an encouraging tone.   3.2
sagte der Märzhase in einem ermutigenden Ton.

Alice looked all round the table,   4.1
Alice sah sich auf dem Tisch um,

but there was nothing on it but tea.   4.2
aber außer Tee war nichts darauf zu finden.

"I don't see any wine," she remarked.   4.3
"Ich sehe keinen Wein," bemerkte sie.

5.1 "There isn't any," said the March Hare.

"Es gibt keine," sagte der Märzhase.

6.1 "Then it wasn't very civil of you to offer it,"

"Dann war es nicht sehr höflich von dir, es anzubieten,"

6.2 said Alice angrily.

sagte Alice verärgert.

7.1 "It wasn't very civil of you to sit down without being invited,"

"Es war nicht sehr höflich von dir, dich unaufgefordert zu setzen,"

7.2 said the March Hare.

sagte der Märzhase.

8.1 "I didn't know it was your table," said Alice;

"Ich wusste nicht, dass es dein Tisch ist," sagte Alice,

8.2 "it's laid for a great many more than three."

"er ist für viel mehr als drei Personen gedeckt."

9.1 "Your hair wants cutting," said the Hatter.

"Dein Haar muss geschnitten werden," sagte der Hutmacher.

9.2 He had been looking at Alice for some time with great curiosity,

Er hatte Alice schon seit einiger Zeit mit großer Neugierde beobachtet,

9.3 and this was his first speech.

und dies war seine erste Rede.

"You should learn not to make personal remarks," 10.1

"Du solltest lernen, keine persönlichen Bemerkungen zu machen,"

Alice said with some severity; "it's very rude." 10.2

sagte Alice mit einiger Strenge, "das ist sehr unhöflich."

The Hatter opened his eyes very wide on hearing this; but all he said was: 11.1

Der Hutmacher riss die Augen weit auf, als er das hörte, aber er sagte nur:

"Why is a raven like a writing- desk?" 11.2

"Warum ist ein Rabe wie ein Schreibtisch?"

"Come, we shall have some fun now!" thought Alice. 12.1

"Komm, jetzt werden wir Spaß haben!" dachte Alice.

"I'm glad they've begun asking riddles. 12.2

"Ich bin froh, dass sie angefangen haben, Rätsel zu stellen.

— I believe I can guess that," she added aloud. 12.3

ich glaube, das kann ich erraten," fügte sie laut hinzu.

"Do you mean that you think you can find out the answer to it?" 13.1

"Meinst du, dass du die Antwort darauf herausfinden kannst?"

said the March Hare. 13.2

fragte der Märzhase.

"Exactly so," said Alice. 14.1

"Genau so," sagte Alice.

15.1 "Then you should say what you mean,"
"Dann solltest du sagen, was du meinst,"

15.2 the March Hare went on.
fuhr der Märzhase fort.

16.1 "I do," Alice hastily replied;
"Das tue ich," antwortete Alice hastig,

16.2 "at least — at least I mean what I say — that's the same thing, you know."
"zumindest meine ich, was ich sage - das ist dasselbe, weißt du."

17.1 "Not the same thing a bit!" said the Hatter.
"Das ist nicht dasselbe!" sagte der Hutmacher.

17.2 "You might just as well say that 'I see what I eat'
"Du könntest genauso gut sagen, dass 'ich sehe, was ich esse'

17.3 is the same thing as 'I eat what I see'!"
dasselbe ist wie 'ich esse, was ich sehe'!"

18.1 "You might just as well say," added the March Hare,
"Man könnte genauso gut sagen," fügte der Märzhase hinzu,

18.2 "that 'I like what I get' is the same thing as
"dass 'ich mag, was ich bekomme' dasselbe ist wie

18.3 'I get what I like'!"
'ich bekomme, was ich mag'!"

"You might just as well say,"   19.1
"Genauso gut könntest du sagen,"

added the Dormouse, who seemed to be talking in his   19.2
sleep,
fügte die Haselmaus hinzu, die im Schlaf zu sprechen
schien,

"that 'I breathe when I sleep' is the same thing as   19.3
"dass 'ich atme, wenn ich schlafe' dasselbe ist wie

'I sleep when I breathe'!"   19.4
'ich schlafe, wenn ich atme'!"

"It is the same thing with you,"   20.1
"Bei dir ist es dasselbe,"

said the Hatter, and here the conversation dropped,   20.2
and the party sat silent for a minute, while Alice
thought over all she could remember about ravens
and writing-desks, which wasn't much.
sagte der Hutmacher, und hier brach das Gespräch ab,
und die Gruppe saß eine Minute lang schweigend da,
während Alice über alles nachdachte, was ihr über Raben
und Schreibtische einfiel, und das war nicht viel.

The Hatter was the first to break the silence.   21.1
Der Hutmacher war der erste, der das Schweigen brach.

"What day of the month is it?"   21.2
"Welcher Tag des Monats ist heute?"

21.3 he said, turning to Alice: he had taken his watch out of his pocket, and was looking at it uneasily, shaking it every now and then, and holding it to his ear.

fragte er und wandte sich an Alice; Er hatte seine Uhr aus der Tasche genommen und betrachtete sie unruhig, schüttelte sie ab und zu und hielt sie an sein Ohr.

22.1 Alice considered a little, and then said "The fourth."

Alice überlegte kurz und sagte dann: "Der vierte."

23.1 "Two days wrong!" sighed the Hatter.

"Zwei Tage falsch!" seufzte der Hutmacher.

23.2 "I told you butter wouldn't suit the works!"

"Ich habe dir doch gesagt, dass Butter nicht ins Werk passt!"

23.3 he added looking angrily at the March Hare.

fügte er hinzu und sah den Märzhasen böse an.

24.1 "It was the best butter," the March Hare meekly replied.

"Es war die beste Butter," antwortete der Märzhase kleinlaut.

25.1 "Yes, but some crumbs must have got in as well,"

"Ja, aber es müssen auch ein paar Krümel hineingekommen sein,"

25.2 the Hatter grumbled:

brummte der Hutmacher:

25.3 "you shouldn't have put it in with the bread- knife."

"Du hättest sie nicht mit dem Brotmesser hineinstecken sollen."

The March Hare took the watch and looked at it   26.1
gloomily: then he dipped it into his cup of tea, and
looked at it again: but he could think of nothing
better to say than his first remark:

Der Märzhase nahm die Uhr und betrachtete sie düster;
dann tauchte er sie in seine Tasse Tee und betrachtete sie
wieder; aber ihm fiel nichts Besseres ein als seine erste
Bemerkung:

"It was the best butter, you know."   26.2

"Das war die beste Butter, weißt du."

Alice had been looking over his shoulder with some   27.1
curiosity.

Alice hatte ihm neugierig über die Schulter geschaut.

"What a funny watch!" she remarked.   27.2

"Was für eine komische Uhr!" bemerkte sie.

"It tells the day of the month, and doesn't tell what   27.3
o'clock it is!"

"Sie zeigt den Tag des Monats an, aber nicht, wie viel Uhr es
ist!"

"Why should it?" muttered the Hatter.   28.1

"Warum sollte sie?" murmelte der Hutmacher.

"Does your watch tell you what year it is?"   28.2

"Sagt dir deine Uhr, welches Jahr wir haben?"

"Of course not," Alice replied very readily: 29.1

"Natürlich nicht," antwortete Alice sehr bereitwillig:

29.2 "but that's because it stays the same year for such a long time together."

"Aber das liegt daran, dass es so lange ein und dasselbe Jahr bleibt."

30.1 "Which is just the case with mine," said the Hatter.

"Das ist genau der Fall bei mir," sagte der Hutmacher.

31.1 Alice felt dreadfully puzzled.

Alice fühlte sich furchtbar verwirrt.

31.2 The Hatter's remark seemed to have no sort of meaning in it,

Die Bemerkung des Hutmachers schien keinen Sinn zu haben,

31.3 and yet it was certainly English.

und doch war sie eindeutig englisch.

31.4 "I don't quite understand you,"

"Ich verstehe Sie nicht ganz,"

31.5 she said, as politely as she could.

sagte sie so höflich wie möglich.

32.1 "The Dormouse is asleep again,"

"Die Haselmaus schläft wieder,"

32.2 said the Hatter, and he poured a little hot tea upon its nose.

sagte der Hutmacher und schüttete ihr ein wenig heißen Tee auf die Nase.

The Dormouse shook its head impatiently, and said, without opening its eyes,

33.1

Die Haselmaus schüttelte ungeduldig den Kopf und sagte, ohne die Augen zu öffnen:

"Of course, of course; just what I was going to remark myself."

33.2

"Natürlich, natürlich; genau das wollte ich auch gerade sagen."

"Have you guessed the riddle yet?"

34.1

"Hast du das Rätsel schon erraten?"

the Hatter said, turning to Alice again.

34.2

sagte der Hutmacher und wandte sich wieder an Alice.

"No, I give it up," Alice replied:

35.1

"Nein, ich gebe es auf," antwortete Alice:

"what's the answer?"

35.2

"Wie lautet die Antwort?"

"I haven't the slightest idea," said the Hatter.

36.1

"Ich habe nicht die geringste Ahnung," sagte der Hutmacher.

"Nor I," said the March Hare.

37.1

"Ich auch nicht," sagte der Märzhase.

Alice sighed wearily.

38.1

Alice seufzte müde.

38.2 **"I think you might do something better with the time,"**
"Ich denke, du könntest etwas Besseres mit deiner Zeit anfangen,"

38.3 **she said,**
sagte sie,

38.4 **"than waste it in asking riddles that have no answers."**
"als sie mit Rätseln zu verschwenden, die keine Antworten haben."

39.1 **"If you knew Time as well as I do,"**
"Wenn du die Zeit so gut kennen würdest wie ich,"

39.2 **said the Hatter,**
sagte der Hutmacher,

39.3 **"you wouldn't talk about wasting it. It's him."**
"würdest du nicht von Zeitverschwendung reden. Er ist es."

40.1 **"I don't know what you mean," said Alice.**
"Ich weiß nicht, was du meinst," sagte Alice.

41.1 **"Of course you don't!"**
"Natürlich nicht!"

41.2 **the Hatter said, tossing his head contemptuously.**
sagte der Hutmacher und warf verächtlich den Kopf herum.

41.3 **"I dare say you never even spoke to Time!"**
"Ich wage zu behaupten, dass du noch nie mit Time gesprochen hast!"

"Perhaps not," Alice cautiously replied:
42.1

"Vielleicht nicht," erwiderte Alice behutsam:

"but I know I have to beat time when I learn music."
42.2

"Aber ich weiß, dass ich die Zeit schlagen muss, wenn ich
Musik lerne."

"Ah! that accounts for it," said the Hatter.
43.1

"Ah! Das erklärt es," sagte der Hutmacher.

"He won't stand beating.
43.2

"Er verträgt keine Schläge.

Now, if you only kept on good terms with him, he'd
43.3
do almost anything you liked with the clock.

Wenn du dich nur gut mit ihm verstehst, wird er mit der
Uhr fast alles machen, was du willst.

For instance, suppose it were nine o'clock in the
43.4
morning, just time to begin lessons:

Nehmen wir zum Beispiel an, es wäre neun Uhr morgens,
gerade Zeit, mit dem Unterricht zu beginnen:

you'd only have to whisper a hint to Time,
43.5

Du müsstest Time nur einen Hinweis zuflüstern,

and round goes the clock in a twinkling! Half-past
43.6
one,

und die Uhr würde sich im Handumdrehen drehen! Halb
zwei,

time for dinner!"
43.7

Zeit zum Essen!"

("I only wish it was,"
44.1

("Ich wünschte nur, es wäre so,"

154

44.2 the March Hare said to itself in a whisper.)
flüsterte der Märzhase zu sich selbst.)

45.1 "That would be grand, certainly," said Alice thoughtfully:
"Das wäre natürlich großartig," sagte Alice nachdenklich:

45.2 "but then — I shouldn't be hungry for it, you know."
"Aber dann hätte ich keinen Hunger darauf, weißt du."

46.1 "Not at first, perhaps," said the Hatter:
"Am Anfang vielleicht nicht," sagte der Hutmacher:

46.2 "but you could keep it to half-past one as long as you liked."
"Aber du kannst es bis halb eins halten, so lange du willst."

47.1 "Is that the way you manage?" Alice asked.
"Ist das die Art und Weise, wie Sie vorgehen?" fragte Alice.

48.1 The Hatter shook his head mournfully. "Not I!"
Der Hutmacher schüttelte bedauernd den Kopf. "Ich nicht!"

48.2 he replied.
antwortete er.

48.3 "We quarrelled last March — just before he went mad, you know — "
"Wir haben uns im letzten März gestritten — kurz bevor er verrückt wurde — "

48.4 (pointing with his tea spoon at the March Hare,)
(er deutete mit seinem Teelöffel auf den Märzhasen)

" — it was at the great concert given by the Queen of Hearts,   48.5
"es war bei dem großen Konzert der Herzkönigin,

and I had to sing   48.6
und ich musste singen

'Twinkle, twinkle, little bat!	Funkelnd, funkelnd, kleine Fledermaus!
How I wonder what you're at!'	Ich frage mich, was du machst!'

You know the song, perhaps?"   50.1
Kennen Sie vielleicht das Lied?"

"I've heard something like it," said Alice.   51.1
"Ich habe so etwas schon gehört," sagte Alice.

"It goes on, you know," the Hatter continued,   52.1
"Es geht, wissen Sie," fuhr der Hutmacher fort,

"in this way:-   52.2
"folgendermaßen weiter:-

'Up above the world you fly,	Hoch über der Welt fliegst du,
Like a tea-tray in the sky.	Wie ein Teetablett im Himmel.
Twinkle, twinkle — "'	Glitzern, glitzern ..."

Here the Dormouse shook itself,   54.1
Da schüttelte sich die Haselmaus und fing an,

54.2 and began singing in its sleep:

im Schlaf zu singen:

54.3 "Twinkle, twinkle, twinkle, twinkle — "

"Glitzern, glitzern, glitzern, glitzern,"

54.4 and went on so long that they had to pinch it to make it stop.

und zwar so lange, dass man sie zwicken musste, damit sie aufhörte.

55.1 "Well, I'd hardly finished the first verse,"

"Nun, ich hatte kaum die erste Strophe beendet,"

55.2 said the Hatter,

sagte der Hutmacher,

55.3 "when the Queen jumped up and bawled out:

"als die Königin aufsprang und brüllte:

55.4 'He's murdering the time! Off with his head! "'

'Er mordet die Zeit! Ab mit seinem Kopf! "'

56.1 "How dreadfully savage!" exclaimed Alice.

"Wie furchtbar wild!" rief Alice aus.

57.1 "And ever since that," the Hatter went on in a mournful tone,

"Und seitdem," fuhr der Hutmacher in traurigem Tonfall fort,

57.2 "he won't do a thing I ask!

"tut er nichts mehr, worum ich ihn bitte!

It's always six o'clock now. "   57.3
Es ist jetzt immer sechs Uhr."

A bright idea came into Alice's head.   58.1
Alice kam eine glänzende Idee in den Kopf.

"Is that the reason so many tea-things are put out   58.2
here?"
"Ist das der Grund, warum hier so viele Teesachen
ausgestellt werden?"

she asked.   58.3
fragte sie.

"Yes, that's it," said the Hatter with a sigh: 59.1
"Ja, das ist es," sagte der Hutmacher mit einem Seufzer:

"it's always tea-time, and we've no time to wash the   59.2
things between whiles."
"Es ist immer Teezeit, und wir haben keine Zeit, die Sachen
zwischendurch zu waschen."

"Then you keep moving round, I suppose?" said Alice.   60.1
"Dann gehst du wohl immer weiter herum?" fragte Alice.

"Exactly so," said the Hatter: 61.1
"Genau so," sagte der Hutmacher:

"as the things get used up."   61.2
"wenn die Sachen aufgebraucht sind."

"But what happens when you come to the beginning   62.1
again?"
"Aber was passiert, wenn man wieder zum Anfang
kommt?"

62.2 **Alice ventured to ask.**
wagte Alice zu fragen.

63.1 **"Suppose we change the subject,"**
"Wechseln wir doch das Thema,"

63.2 **the March Hare interrupted, yawning.**
unterbrach der Märzhase und gähnte.

63.3 **"I'm getting tired of this.**
"Ich habe es langsam satt.

63.4 **I vote the young lady tells us a story."**
Ich bin dafür, dass die junge Dame uns eine Geschichte erzählt."

64.1 **"I'm afraid I don't know one," said Alice,**
"Ich fürchte, ich kenne keinen," sagte Alice,

64.2 **rather alarmed at the proposal.**
etwas erschrocken über diesen Vorschlag.

65.1 **"Then the Dormouse shall!" they both cried. "Wake up,**
"Dann soll die Haselmaus!" riefen beide. "Aufwachen,

65.2 **Dormouse!"**
Haselmaus!"

65.3 **And they pinched it on both sides at once.**
Und sie zwickten sie auf beiden Seiten gleichzeitig.

66.1 **The Dormouse slowly opened his eyes.**
Der Siebenschläfer öffnete langsam seine Augen.

"I wasn't asleep," he said in a hoarse, 66.2

"Ich habe nicht geschlafen," sagte er mit heiserer,

feeble voice: 66.3

schwacher Stimme:

"I heard every word you fellows were saying." 66.4

"Ich habe jedes Wort gehört, das ihr gesagt habt."

"Tell us a story!" said the March Hare. 67.1

"Erzähl uns eine Geschichte!" sagte der Märzhase.

"Yes, please do!" pleaded Alice. 68.1

"Ja, bitte!" flehte Alice.

"And be quick about it," added the Hatter, 69.1

"Und mach schnell," fügte der Hutmacher hinzu,

"or you'll be asleep again before it's done." 69.2

"sonst schläfst du wieder, bevor es erledigt ist."

"Once upon a time there were three little sisters," 70.1

"Es waren einmal drei kleine Schwestern,"

the Dormouse began in a great hurry; 70.2

begann die Haselmaus in großer Eile,

"and their names were Elsie, Lacie, and Tillie; and 70.3
they lived at the bottom of a well — "

"sie hießen Elsie, Lacie und Tillie und lebten auf dem
Grund eines Brunnen — "

"What did they live on?" said Alice, 71.1

"Wovon haben sie gelebt?" fragte Alice,

71.2 **who always took a great interest in questions of eating and drinking.**
die sich schon immer sehr für Fragen des Essens und Trinkens interessierte.

72.1 **"They lived on treacle," said the Dormouse,**
"Sie lebten von Sirup," sagte die Haselmaus,

72.2 **after thinking a minute or two.**
nachdem sie ein oder zwei Minuten nachgedacht hatte.

73.1 **"They couldn't have done that, you know,"**
"Das hätten sie nicht tun können, weißt du,"

73.2 **Alice gently remarked; "they'd have been ill."**
bemerkte Alice sanft, "sie wären krank gewesen."

74.1 **"So they were," said the Dormouse; "very ill."**
"Das waren sie," sagte die Haselmaus, "sehr krank."

75.1 **Alice tried to fancy to herself what such an extraordinary ways of living would be like, but it puzzled her too much, so she went on:**
Alice versuchte, sich vorzustellen, wie eine so außergewöhnliche Lebensweise aussehen könnte, aber es verwirrte sie zu sehr, also fuhr sie fort:

75.2 **"But why did they live at the bottom of a well?"**
"Aber warum haben sie auf dem Grund eines Brunnens gelebt?"

76.1 **"Take some more tea," the March Hare said to Alice,**
"Nimm noch etwas Tee," sagte der Märzhase zu Alice,

very earnestly.   76.2
sehr ernst.

"I've had nothing yet,"   77.1
"Ich habe noch nichts getrunken,"

Alice replied in an offended tone,   77.2
antwortete Alice in einem beleidigten Ton,

"so I can't take more."   77.3
"also kann ich nicht mehr nehmen."

"You mean you can't take less,"   78.1
"Du meinst, du kannst nicht weniger nehmen,"

said the Hatter: 78.2
sagte der Hutmacher:

"it's very easy to take more than nothing."   78.3
"Es ist sehr einfach, mehr als nichts zu nehmen."

"Nobody asked your opinion," said Alice.   79.1
"Niemand hat dich nach deiner Meinung gefragt," sagte
Alice.

"Who's making personal remarks now?"   80.1
"Wer macht jetzt persönliche Bemerkungen?"

the Hatter asked triumphantly.   80.2
fragte der Hutmacher triumphierend.

81.1 Alice did not quite know what to say to this: so she helped herself to some tea and bread-and-butter, and then turned to the Dormouse, and repeated her question.

Alice wusste nicht recht, was sie dazu sagen sollte, und so nahm sie sich etwas Tee und Brot und Butter, wandte sich dann an die Haselmaus und wiederholte ihre Frage.

81.2 "Why did they live at the bottom of a well?"

"Warum haben sie auf dem Grund eines Brunnens gelebt?"

82.1 The Dormouse again took a minute or two to think about it, and then said:

Die Haselmaus brauchte wieder ein oder zwei Minuten, um darüber nachzudenken, und sagte dann:

82.2 "It was a treacle- well."

"Es war ein Sirup- Brunnen."

83.1 "There's no such thing!" Alice was beginning very angrily,

"So etwas gibt es nicht!" Alice begann sehr wütend,

83.2 but the Hatter and the March Hare went "Sh! sh!"

aber der Hutmacher und der Märzhase machten "Pst! Pst!"

83.3 and the Dormouse sulkily remarked:

und die Haselmaus bemerkte mürrisch:

83.4 "If you can't be civil,

"Wenn du nicht höflich sein kannst,

83.5 you'd better finish the story for yourself."

solltest du die Geschichte besser selbst zu Ende erzählen."

"No, please go on!" Alice said very humbly;   84.1
"Nein, bitte fahren Sie fort!" sagte Alice sehr bescheiden;

"I won't interrupt again.   84.2
"ich werde nicht mehr unterbrechen.

I dare say there may be one."   84.3
Ich wage zu behaupten, dass es einen geben könnte."

"One, indeed!" said the Dormouse indignantly.   85.1
"Ja, eine!" sagte die Haselmaus entrüstet.

However, he consented to go on.   85.2
Er willigte jedoch ein, fortzufahren.

"And so these three little sisters -   85.3
"Und diese drei kleinen Schwestern -

they were learning to draw, you know -"   85.4
sie lernten malen, wisst ihr -"

"What did they draw?"   86.1
"Was haben sie gezeichnet?"

said Alice, quite forgetting her promise.   86.2
fragte Alice und vergaß dabei ihr Versprechen.

"Treacle," said the Dormouse,   87.1
"Sirup," sagte die Haselmaus,

without considering at all this time.   87.2
ohne zu überlegen.

88.1 "I want a clean cup," interrupted the Hatter:
"Ich will eine saubere Tasse," unterbrach ihn der Hutmacher:

88.2 "let's all move one place on."
"Lasst uns alle einen Platz weitergehen."

89.1 He moved on as he spoke, and the Dormouse followed him:
Er ging weiter, während er sprach, und die Haselmaus folgte ihm:

89.2 the March Hare moved into the Dormouse's place,
der Märzhase nahm den Platz der Haselmaus ein,

89.3 and Alice rather unwillingly took the place of the March Hare.
und Alice nahm eher widerwillig den Platz des Märzhasen ein.

89.4 The Hatter was the only one who got any advantage from the change: and Alice was a good deal worse off than before, as the March Hare had just upset the milk-jug into his plate.
Der Hutmacher war der Einzige, der von dem Wechsel profitierte, und Alice war viel schlechter dran als vorher, denn der Märzhase hatte ihm gerade das Milchkännchen in den Teller gekippt.

90.1 Alice did not wish to offend the Dormouse again,
Alice wollte die Haselmaus nicht noch einmal beleidigen,

90.2 so she began very cautiously:
also begann sie sehr vorsichtig:

90.3 "But I don't understand.
"Aber das verstehe ich nicht.

Where did they draw the treacle from?"

90.4

Woher haben sie den Sirup genommen?"

"You can draw water out of a water- well,"

91.1

"Du kannst Wasser aus einem Wasserbrunnen schöpfen,"

said the Hatter;

91.2

sagte der Hutmacher,

"so I should think you could draw treacle out of a treacle-well — eh, stupid."

91.3

"also denke ich, dass du auch Sirup aus einem Sirupbrunnen schöpfen kannst, du Dummkopf."

"But they were in the well," Alice said to the Dormouse,

92.1

"Aber sie waren doch im Brunnen," sagte Alice zu der Haselmaus,

not choosing to notice this last remark.

92.2

die diese letzte Bemerkung nicht bemerkte.

"Of course they were," said the Dormouse;

93.1

"Natürlich waren sie das," sagte die Haselmaus,

" — well in."

93.2

"und das ist gut so."

This answer so confused poor Alice, that she let the Dormouse go on for some time without interrupting it.

94.1

Diese Antwort verwirrte die arme Alice so sehr, dass sie die Haselmaus noch eine Weile weitermachen ließ, ohne sie zu unterbrechen.

95.1 "They were learning to draw,"

"Sie haben zeichnen gelernt,"

95.2 the Dormouse went on, yawning and rubbing its eyes, for it was getting very sleepy;

fuhr die Haselmaus fort, gähnte und rieb sich die Augen, denn sie wurde sehr müde,

95.3 "and they drew all manner of things — everything that begins with an M — "

"und sie haben alles Mögliche gezeichnet - alles, was mit einem M beginnt..."

96.1 "Why with an M?" said Alice.

"Warum mit M?" fragte Alice.

97.1 "Why not?" said the March Hare.

"Warum nicht?" sagte der Märzhase.

98.1 Alice was silent.

Alice war still.

99.1 The Dormouse had closed its eyes by this time, and was going off into a doze;

Die Haselmaus hatte inzwischen die Augen geschlossen und döste vor sich hin;

99.2 but, on being pinched by the Hatter, it woke up again with a little shriek, and went on:

aber als sie von dem Hutmacher gezwickt wurde, wachte sie mit einem kleinen Schrei wieder auf und fuhr fort:

" — that begins with an M, such as mouse-traps, and the moon, and memory, and muchness — you know you say things are "much of a muchness" — did you ever see such a thing as a drawing of a muchness?"   99.3

"Was mit M anfängt, wie Mausefallen und der Mond und das Gedächtnis und die Vielheit - du weißt doch, dass man sagt, die Dinge seien "viel von einer Vielheit" - hast du jemals so etwas wie eine Zeichnung von einer Vielheit gesehen?"

"Really, now you ask me,"   100.1

"Wirklich, jetzt wo du mich fragst,"

said Alice, very much confused, "I don't think — "   100.2

sagte Alice, sehr verwirrt, "ich glaube nicht — "

"Then you shouldn't talk," said the Hatter.   101.1

"Dann solltest du nicht reden," sagte der Hutmacher.

This piece of rudeness was more than Alice could bear: 102.1

Diese Unhöflichkeit war mehr, als Alice ertragen konnte:

she got up in great disgust, and walked off;   102.2

sie stand empört auf und ging weg;

the Dormouse fell asleep instantly, and neither of the others took the least notice of her going, though she looked back once or twice, half hoping that they would call after her: 102.3

die Haselmaus schlief sofort ein, und keiner der anderen nahm Notiz von ihrem Weggang, obwohl sie ein - oder zweimal zurückschaute, halb in der Hoffnung, dass sie nach ihr rufen würden:

102.4 the last time she saw them, they were trying to put the Dormouse into the teapot.
als sie sie das letzte Mal sah, versuchten sie, die Haselmaus in die Teekanne zu stecken.

103.1 "At any rate I'll never go there again!"
"Ich werde auf jeden Fall nie wieder hingehen,"

103.2 said Alice as she picked her way through the wood.
sagte Alice, während sie sich ihren Weg durch den Wald bahnte.

103.3 "It's the stupidest tea-party I ever was at in all my life!"
"Das ist die dümmste Teeparty, auf der ich je in meinem Leben war!"

104.1 Just as she said this, she noticed that one of the trees had a door leading right into it.
Gerade als sie dies sagte, bemerkte sie, dass einer der Bäume eine Tür hatte, die direkt in ihn hineinführte.

104.2 "That's very curious!" she thought.
"Das ist sehr seltsam!" dachte sie.

104.3 "But everything's curious today.
"Aber heute ist alles seltsam.

104.4 I think I may as well go in at once."
Ich denke, ich kann auch gleich hineingehen."

104.5 And in she went.
Und so ging sie hinein.

Once more she found herself in the long hall, and close to the little glass table. 105.1

Sie fand sich wieder in der langen Halle und in der Nähe des kleinen Glastisches.

"Now, I'll manage better this time," 105.2

"Diesmal werde ich es besser machen,"

she said to herself, and began by taking the little golden key, and unlocking the door that led into the garden. 105.3

sagte sie zu sich selbst und begann, den kleinen goldenen Schlüssel zu nehmen und die Tür aufzuschließen, die in den Garten führte.

Then she went to work nibbling at the mushroom (she had kept a piece of it in her pocket) till she was about a foot high: then she walked down the little passage: and then - 105.4

Dann machte sie sich an die Arbeit und knabberte an dem Pilz (sie hatte ein Stück davon in ihrer Tasche aufbewahrt), bis sie etwa einen Fuß hoch war; dann ging sie den kleinen Gang hinunter: und dann -

she found herself at last in the beautiful garden, 105.5

fand sie sich endlich in dem schönen Garten wieder,

among the bright flower-beds and the cool fountains. 105.6

zwischen den leuchtenden Blumenbeeten und den kühlen Springbrunnen.

CHAPTER VIII. The Queen's Croquet-Ground

KAPITEL VIII. Der Krocketplatz der Königin

1.1 A large rose-tree stood near the entrance of the garden: the roses growing on it were white, but there were three gardeners at it, busily painting them red.

Am Eingang des Gartens stand ein großer Rosenbaum, an dem weiße Rosen wuchsen, aber drei Gärtner waren damit beschäftigt, sie rot anzumalen.

1.2 Alice thought this a very curious thing, and she went nearer to watch them, and just as she came up to them she heard one of them say:

Alice fand das sehr merkwürdig und ging näher heran, um sie zu beobachten, und gerade als sie auf sie zukam, hörte sie einen von ihnen sagen:

1.3 "Look out now, Five!

"Pass auf, Fünf!

1.4 Don't go splashing paint over me like that!"

Spritzt nicht so mit Farbe über mich!"

"I couldn't help it," said Five, in a sulky tone; 2.1

"Ich konnte nicht anders," sagte Fünf in einem mürrischen Ton;

"Seven jogged my elbow." 2.2

"Sieben hat meinen Ellbogen geschüttelt."

On which Seven looked up and said, "That's right, Five! 3.1

Daraufhin blickte Seven auf und sagte: "Das stimmt, Five!

Always lay the blame on others!" 3.2

Schieb die Schuld immer auf andere!"

"You'd better not talk!" said Five. 4.1

"Du solltest besser nicht reden!" sagte Fünf.

"I heard the Queen say only yesterday you deserved to be beheaded!" 4.2

"Ich habe erst gestern gehört, wie die Königin sagte, dass du es verdienst, geköpft zu werden!"

"What for?" said the one who had spoken first. 5.1

"Wozu?" fragte derjenige, der zuerst gesprochen hatte.

"That's none of your business, Two!" said Seven. 6.1

"Das geht dich nichts an, Zwei!" sagte Seven.

"Yes, it is his business!" said Five, 7.1

"Ja, das ist seine Sache!" sagte Fünf,

7.2 "and I'll tell him — it was for bringing the cook tulip-roots instead of onions."

"und ich werde ihm sagen, dass er der Köchin Tulpenzwiebeln statt Zwiebeln gebracht hat."

8.1 Seven flung down his brush, and had just begun "Well, of all the unjust things — " when his eye chanced to fall upon Alice, as she stood watching them, and he checked himself suddenly:

Seven warf den Pinsel weg und hatte gerade begonnen:

8.2 the others looked round also, and all of them bowed low.

"Was für eine Ungerechtigkeit!" als sein Blick zufällig auf Alice fiel, die sie beobachtete, und er hielt sich plötzlich zurück.

9.1 "Would you tell me," said Alice, a little timidly,

"Würdest du mir sagen," sagte Alice ein wenig zaghaft,

9.2 "why you are painting those roses?"

"warum du diese Rosen malst?"

10.1 Five and Seven said nothing, but looked at Two.

Fünf und Sieben sagten nichts, sondern sahen Zwei an.

10.2 Two began in a low voice,

Zwei begann mit leiser Stimme:

10.3 "Why the fact is, you see, Miss, this here ought to have been a red rose-tree, and we put a white one in by mistake;

"Sehen Sie, Fräulein, das hier sollte eigentlich ein roter Rosenstock sein, und wir haben aus Versehen einen weißen hineingesteckt;

and if the Queen was to find it out, we should all have our heads cut off, you know.   10.4

und wenn die Königin das herausfindet, werden wir alle geköpft, wissen Sie.

So you see, Miss, we're doing our best, afore she comes, to — "   10.5

Sie sehen also, Fräulein, wir tun unser Bestes, bevor sie kommt, um — "

At this moment Five, who had been anxiously looking across the garden, called out,   10.6

In diesem Augenblick rief Fünf, der ängstlich durch den Garten geschaut hatte,

"The Queen! The Queen!"   10.7

"Die Königin! Die Königin!"

and the three gardeners instantly threw themselves flat upon their faces.   10.8

und die drei Gärtner warfen sich augenblicklich auf ihr Gesicht.

There was a sound of many footsteps, and Alice looked round, eager to see the Queen.   10.9

Es ertönten viele Schritte, und Alice schaute sich um, um die Königin zu sehen.

First came ten soldiers carrying clubs;   11.1

Zuerst kamen zehn Soldaten, die Keulen trugen;

these were all shaped like the three gardeners, oblong and flat, with their hands and feet at the corners: 11.2

sie waren alle so geformt wie die drei Gärtner, länglich und flach, mit ihren Händen und Füßen an den Ecken:

11.3 **next the ten courtiers;**
dann die zehn Höflinge;

11.4 **these were ornamented all over with diamonds, and walked two and two, as the soldiers did.**
diese waren über und über mit Diamanten verziert und gingen zu zweit, wie die Soldaten.

11.5 **After these came the royal children;**
Nach diesen kamen die königlichen Kinder, zehn an der Zahl, und die kleinen Lieblinge hüpften fröhlich Hand in Hand, in Paaren;

11.6 **there were ten of them, and the little dears came jumping merrily along hand in hand, in couples: they were all ornamented with hearts.**
sie waren alle mit Herzen geschmückt.

11.7 **Next came the guests, mostly Kings and Queens, and among them Alice recognised the White Rabbit:**
Als nächstes kamen die Gäste, meist Könige und Königinnen, und unter ihnen erkannte Alice das weiße Kaninchen:

11.8 **it was talking in a hurried nervous manner, smiling at everything that was said, and went by without noticing her.**
es sprach eilig und nervös, lächelte über alles, was gesagt wurde, und ging an ihr vorbei, ohne sie zu beachten.

Then followed the Knave of Hearts, carrying the 11.9
King's crown on a crimson velvet cushion; and, last
of all this grand procession, came THE KING AND
QUEEN OF HEARTS.

Dann folgte der Herzbube, der die Krone des Königs auf
einem karmesinroten Samtkissen trug, und als letzter in
dieser großen Prozession kamen DER KÖNIG UND DIE
KÖNIGIN DER HERZEN.

Alice was rather doubtful whether she ought not to 12.1
lie down on her face like the three gardeners, but she
could not remember ever having heard of such a rule
at processions;

Alice war etwas unsicher, ob sie sich nicht wie die drei
Gärtner auf das Gesicht legen sollte, aber sie konnte
sich nicht erinnern, jemals von einer solchen Regel bei
Prozessionen gehört zu haben;

"and besides, what would be the use of a procession," 12.2

"und außerdem, was hätte eine Prozession für einen Sinn,"

thought she, 12.3

dachte sie,

"if people had all to lie down upon their faces, 12.4

"wenn sich alle auf das Gesicht legen müssten,

so that they couldn't see it?" 12.5

damit man sie nicht sehen könnte?"

So she stood still where she was, and waited. 12.6

Sie blieb also stehen, wo sie war, und wartete.

176

13.1 When the procession came opposite to Alice, they all stopped and looked at her, and the Queen said severely:

Als die Prozession Alice gegenüberstand, blieben alle stehen und sahen sie an, und die Königin sagte ernst:

13.2 "Who is this?" She said it to the Knave of Hearts,

"Wer ist das?" Sie sagte es zu dem Herzbuben,

13.3 who only bowed and smiled in reply.

der sich nur verbeugte und lächelte.

14.1 "Idiot!" said the Queen, tossing her head impatiently;

"Idiot!" sagte die Königin und schüttelte ungeduldig den Kopf;

14.2 and, turning to Alice, she went on, "What's your name,

dann wandte sie sich an Alice und fuhr fort, "Wie heißt du,

14.3 child?"

Kind?"

15.1 "My name is Alice, so please your Majesty,"

"Ich heiße Alice, also bitte, Eure Majestät,"

15.2 said Alice very politely; but she added, to herself:

sagte Alice sehr höflich, aber sie fügte hinzu:

15.3 "Why, they're only a pack of cards, after all.

"Es ist doch nur ein Kartenspiel.

15.4 I needn't be afraid of them!"

Ich brauche keine Angst vor ihnen zu haben!"

"And who are these?"   16.1
"Und wer sind die?"

said the Queen,   16.2
fragte die Königin und deutete auf die drei Gärtner,

pointing to the three gardeners who were lying   16.3
round the rose-tree;
die um den Rosenstock herumlagen;

for, you see, as they were lying on their faces, and the   16.4
pattern on their backs was the same as the rest of the
pack, she could not tell whether they were gardeners,
or soldiers, or courtiers, or three of her own children.
denn da sie auf dem Gesicht lagen und das Muster auf
ihrem Rücken dasselbe war wie das der übrigen Meute,
konnte sie nicht sagen, ob es Gärtner, Soldaten, Höflinge
oder drei ihrer eigenen Kinder waren.

"How should I know?" said Alice,   17.1
"Woher soll ich das wissen?" sagte Alice,

surprised at her own courage.   17.2
überrascht über ihren eigenen Mut.

"It's no business of mine."   17.3
"Es geht mich nichts an."

The Queen turned crimson with fury, and, after   18.1
glaring at her for a moment like a wild beast,
screamed:
Die Königin wurde rot vor Wut und schrie, nachdem sie sie
einen Moment lang wie eine wilde Bestie angestarrt hatte:

"Off with her head! Off — "   18.2
"Ab mit ihrem Kopf! Ab — "

19.1 **"Nonsense!"**

"Unsinn!"

19.2 **said Alice, very loudly and decidedly, and the Queen was silent.**

sagte Alice sehr laut und entschieden, und die Königin schwieg.

20.1 **The King laid his hand upon her arm, and timidly said "Consider, my dear:**

Der König legte seine Hand auf ihren Arm und sagte zaghaft:

20.2 **she is only a child!"**

"Bedenke, meine Liebe, sie ist noch ein Kind!"

21.1 **The Queen turned angrily away from him, and said to the Knave:**

Die Königin wandte sich zornig von ihm ab und sagte zu dem Knappen:

21.2 **"Turn them over!"**

"Gib sie her!"

22.1 **The Knave did so, very carefully, with one foot.**

Der Knappe tat dies, sehr vorsichtig, mit einem Fuß.

23.1 **"Get up!"**

"Steh auf!"

said the Queen, in a shrill, loud voice, and the three gardeners instantly jumped up, and began bowing to the King, the Queen, the royal children, and everybody else.

23.2

sagte die Königin mit schriller, lauter Stimme, und die drei Gärtner sprangen sofort auf und verbeugten sich vor dem König, der Königin, den Königskindern und allen anderen.

"Leave off that!" screamed the Queen.

24.1

"Lassen Sie das!" schrie die Königin.

"You make me giddy."

24.2

"Du machst mich schwindlig."

And then, turning to the rose-tree, she went on:

24.3

Dann wandte sie sich dem Rosenstock zu und fuhr fort:

"What have you been doing here?"

24.4

"Was hast du hier gemacht?"

"May it please your Majesty,"

25.1

"Möge es Eurer Majestät gefallen,"

said Two, in a very humble tone, going down on one knee as he spoke,

25.2

sagte Zwei in einem sehr bescheidenen Ton und ging dabei auf ein Knie,

"we were trying — "

25.3

"wir haben versucht — "

"I see!" said the Queen,

26.1

"Ich verstehe," sagte die Königin,

who had meanwhile been examining the roses.

26.2

die inzwischen die Rosen begutachtet hatte.

26.3 "Off with their heads!"

"Ab mit ihren Köpfen!"

26.4 and the procession moved on, three of the soldiers remaining behind to execute the unfortunate gardeners, who ran to Alice for protection.

und der Zug setzte sich in Bewegung, wobei drei der Soldaten zurückblieben, um die unglücklichen Gärtner zu exekutieren, die zu Alice liefen, um sie zu schützen.

27.1 "You shan't be beheaded!"

"Ihr werdet nicht geköpft!"

27.2 said Alice,

sagte Alice und legte sie in einen großen Blumentopf,

27.3 and she put them into a large flower-pot that stood near.

der in der Nähe stand.

27.4 The three soldiers wandered about for a minute or two, looking for them, and then quietly marched off after the others.

Die drei Soldaten irrten ein oder zwei Minuten lang umher, um sie zu suchen, und marschierten dann leise hinter den anderen her.

28.1 "Are their heads off?" shouted the Queen.

"Sind die Köpfe ab?" rief die Königin.

29.1 "Their heads are gone, if it please your Majesty!"

"Ihre Köpfe sind weg, wenn es Eurer Majestät recht ist!"

29.2 the soldiers shouted in reply.

riefen die Soldaten als Antwort.

"That's right!" shouted the Queen.   30.1

"Das stimmt!" rief die Königin.

"Can you play croquet?"   30.2

"Kannst du Krocket spielen?"

The soldiers were silent, and looked at Alice, as the   31.1
question was evidently meant for her.

Die Soldaten schwiegen und sahen Alice an, da die Frage
offensichtlich an sie gerichtet war.

"Yes!" shouted Alice.   32.1

"Ja!" rief Alice.

"Come on, then!"   33.1

"Komm schon!"

roared the Queen, and Alice joined the procession,   33.2
wondering very much what would happen next.

brüllte die Königin, und Alice schloss sich dem Zug an,
wobei sie sich sehr fragte, was wohl als Nächstes passieren
würde.

"It's — it's a very fine day."   34.1

"Es ist ein sehr schöner Tag."

said a timid voice at her side.   34.2

sagte eine ängstliche Stimme neben ihr.

She was walking by the White Rabbit,   34.3

Sie ging neben dem weißen Kaninchen her,

who was peeping anxiously into her face.   34.4

das ihr ängstlich ins Gesicht blickte.

35.1 "Very," said Alice: " — where's the Duchess?"
"Sehr," sagte Alice: " — wo ist die Herzogin?"

36.1 "Hush! Hush!" said the Rabbit in a low,
"Still! Still!" sagte das Kaninchen mit leiser,

36.2 hurried tone.
hastiger Stimme.

36.3 He looked anxiously over his shoulder as he spoke,
and then raised himself upon tiptoe, put his mouth
close to her ear, and whispered:
Er schaute ängstlich über seine Schulter, während er
sprach, dann stellte er sich auf die Zehenspitzen, hielt
seinen Mund dicht an ihr Ohr und flüsterte:

36.4 "She's under sentence of execution."
"Sie ist zur Hinrichtung verurteilt."

37.1 "What for?" said Alice.
"Wozu?" fragte Alice.

38.1 "Did you say 'What a pity!' ?" the Rabbit asked.
"Hast du 'Schade!' gesagt?" fragte das Kaninchen.

39.1 "No, I didn't," said Alice:
"Nein, habe ich nicht," sagte Alice:

39.2 "I don't think it's at all a pity. I said 'What for? "'
"Ich finde das überhaupt nicht schade. Ich sagte: 'Wozu? "'

40.1 "She boxed the Queen's ears — " the Rabbit began.
"Sie hat der Königin die Ohren geboxt," begann das
Kaninchen.

Alice gave a little scream of laughter. "Oh, hush!" 40.2
Alice stieß einen kleinen Lachschrei aus. "Oh, still!"

the Rabbit whispered in a frightened tone. 40.3
flüsterte das Kaninchen in einem ängstlichen Ton.

"The Queen will hear you! 40.4
"Die Königin wird dich hören!

You see, she came rather late, and the Queen said — " 40.5
Sie kam nämlich ziemlich spät, und die Königin sagte — "

"Get to your places!" 41.1
"Auf eure Plätze!"

shouted the Queen in a voice of thunder, and people 41.2
began running about in all directions, tumbling up
against each other;
rief die Königin mit Donnerstimme, und die Leute
begannen, in alle Richtungen zu rennen und sich
gegenseitig zu stoßen;

however, they got settled down in a minute or two, 41.3
and the game began.
aber in ein oder zwei Minuten hatten sie sich wieder
beruhigt, und das Spiel begann.

Alice thought she had never seen such a curious 41.4
croquet-ground in her life;
Alice glaubte, noch nie in ihrem Leben einen so
merkwürdigen Krocketplatz gesehen zu haben;

it was all ridges and furrows; 41.5
er bestand aus lauter Erhebungen und Furchen;

41.6 the balls were live hedgehogs, the mallets live flamingoes, and the soldiers had to double themselves up and to stand on their hands and feet, to make the arches.

die Bälle waren lebende Igel, die Schläger lebende Flamingos, und die Soldaten mussten sich verdoppeln und auf Händen und Füßen stehen, um die Bögen zu bilden.

42.1 The chief difficulty Alice found at first was in managing her flamingo:

Die größte Schwierigkeit, die Alice anfangs hatte, bestand darin, ihren Flamingo in den Griff zu bekommen:

42.2 she succeeded in getting its body tucked away, comfortably enough, under her arm, with its legs hanging down, but generally, just as she had got its neck nicely straightened out, and was going to give the hedgehog a blow with its head, it would twist itself round and look up in her face, with such a puzzled expression that she could not help bursting out laughing:

Es gelang ihr, seinen Körper bequem unter ihren Arm zu klemmen, wobei die Beine nach unten hingen, aber in der Regel drehte sich der Igel gerade dann, wenn sie seinen Hals schön aufgerichtet hatte und ihm einen Schlag mit dem Kopf versetzen wollte, um die eigene Achse und schaute ihr mit einem so verwirrten Gesichtsausdruck ins Gesicht, dass sie nicht anders konnte, als in Gelächter auszubrechen:

and when she had got its head down, and was going
to begin again, it was very provoking to find that the
hedgehog had unrolled itself, and was in the act of
crawling away:

42.3

Und wenn sie den Kopf wieder heruntergenommen hatte
und von vorn beginnen wollte, war es sehr ärgerlich,
dass der Igel sich entrollt hatte und gerade dabei war,
wegzukriechen:

besides all this, there was generally a ridge or
furrow in the way wherever she wanted to send the
hedgehog to, and, as the doubled-up soldiers were
always getting up and walking off to other parts of
the ground, Alice soon came to the conclusion that it
was a very difficult game indeed.

42.4

Außerdem war überall dort, wo sie den Igel hinschicken
wollte, ein Grat oder eine Furche im Weg, und da die
verdoppelten Soldaten immer wieder aufstanden und
an andere Stellen des Bodens liefen, kam Alice bald zu dem
Schluss, dass das Spiel wirklich sehr schwierig war.

The players all played at once without waiting for
turns, quarrelling all the while, and fighting for the
hedgehogs;

43.1

Die Spieler spielten alle auf einmal, ohne zu warten, bis
sie an der Reihe waren, zankten sich die ganze Zeit und
kämpften um die Igel;

and in a very short time the Queen was in a furious
passion, and went stamping about, and shouting

43.2

und in kürzester Zeit war die Königin in heller Aufregung,
stampfte herum und rief etwa einmal in der Minute

"Off with his head!" or "Off with her head!" about
once in a minute.

43.3

"Ab mit seinem Kopf!" oder "Ab mit ihrem Kopf!".

44.1 Alice began to feel very uneasy:
Alice wurde sehr unruhig:

44.2 to be sure, she had not as yet had any dispute with
the Queen, but she knew that it might happen any
minute,
Zwar hatte sie noch keinen Streit mit der Königin gehabt,
aber sie wusste, dass es jeden Moment dazu kommen
konnte,

44.3 "and then," thought she, "what would
become of me?
"und dann," dachte sie, "was würde dann aus mir werden?

44.4 They're dreadfully fond of beheading people here;
Die Leute werden hier furchtbar gern enthauptet;

44.5 the great wonder is, that there's any one left alive!"
das große Wunder ist, dass überhaupt noch jemand am
Leben ist!"

45.1 She was looking about for some way of escape, and
wondering whether she could get away without being
seen, when she noticed a curious appearance in
the air: it puzzled her very much at first, but, after
watching it a minute or two, she made it out to be a
grin, and she said to herself:
Sie schaute sich nach einem Fluchtweg um und fragte
sich, ob sie ungesehen entkommen könnte, als sie eine
seltsame Erscheinung in der Luft bemerkte: Sie verwirrte
sie zuerst sehr, aber nachdem sie sie ein oder zwei Minuten
beobachtet hatte, erkannte sie, dass es sich um ein Grinsen
handelte, und sagte zu sich selbst:

45.2 "It's the Cheshire Cat:
"Es ist die Grinsekatze:

now I shall have somebody to talk to."   45.3

Jetzt werde ich jemanden haben, mit dem ich reden kann."

"How are you getting on?"   46.1

"Wie kommst du voran?"

said the Cat, as soon as there was mouth enough for it   46.2
to speak with.

fragte die Katze, sobald sie einen Mund hatte, mit dem sie
sprechen konnte.

Alice waited till the eyes appeared, and then nodded.   47.1

Alice wartete, bis die Augen erschienen, und nickte dann.

"It's no use speaking to it," she thought,   47.2

"Es hat keinen Sinn, mit ihm zu sprechen," dachte sie,

"till its ears have come, or at least one of them."   47.3

"bis die Ohren da sind, oder zumindest eines davon."

In another minute the whole head appeared, and   47.4
then Alice put down her flamingo, and began an
account of the game, feeling very glad she had
someone to listen to her.

Nach einer weiteren Minute erschien der ganze Kopf, und
dann setzte Alice ihren Flamingo ab und begann, von dem
Spiel zu erzählen, wobei sie sehr froh war, dass ihr jemand
zuhörte.

The Cat seemed to think that there was enough of it   47.5
now in sight, and no more of it appeared.

Die Katze schien der Meinung zu sein, dass sie nun genug
gesehen hatte, und es erschien nichts mehr von ihr.

"I don't think they play at all fairly,"   48.1

"Ich finde, sie spielen überhaupt nicht fair,"

188

48.2 Alice began, in rather a complaining tone,
begann Alice in einem ziemlich beschwerlichen Ton,

48.3 "and they all quarrel so dreadfully one can't hear oneself speak — and they don't seem to have any rules in particular;
"und sie streiten sich alle so furchtbar, dass man sich selbst nicht sprechen hören kann — und sie scheinen keine besonderen Regeln zu haben;

48.4 at least, if there are, nobody attends to them — and you've no idea how confusing it is all the things being alive;
zumindest, wenn es welche gibt, hält sich niemand daran — und du kannst dir nicht vorstellen, wie verwirrend es ist, dass alle Dinge lebendig sind;

48.5 for instance, there's the arch I've got to go through next walking about at the other end of the ground — and I should have croqueted the Queen's hedgehog just now, only it ran away when it saw mine coming!"
Da ist zum Beispiel der Bogen, durch den ich als nächstes gehen muss, wenn ich am anderen Ende des Geländes herumlaufe, und ich hätte gerade den Igel der Königin krocketieren sollen, aber er lief weg, als er meinen kommen sah!"

49.1 "How do you like the Queen?"
"Wie gefällt dir die Königin?"

49.2 said the Cat in a low voice.
fragte die Katze mit leiser Stimme.

50.1 "Not at all," said Alice: "she's so extremely — "
"Ganz und gar nicht," sagte Alice, "sie ist so extrem — "

Just then she noticed that the Queen was close behind her, listening: so she went on,
50.2

In diesem Moment bemerkte sie, dass die Königin dicht hinter ihr stand und zuhörte, und fuhr fort,

" — likely to win, that it's hardly worth while finishing the game."
50.3

"Die Wahrscheinlichkeit, dass sie gewinnt, ist so groß, dass es sich kaum lohnt, das Spiel zu beenden."

The Queen smiled and passed on.
51.1

Die Königin lächelte und ging weiter.

"Who are you talking to?"
52.1

"Mit wem sprichst du?"

said the King, going up to Alice, and looking at the Cat's head with great curiosity.
52.2

fragte der König, ging auf Alice zu und betrachtete den Kopf der Katze mit großer Neugierde.

"It's a friend of mine — a Cheshire Cat," said Alice:
53.1

"Es ist ein Freund von mir, eine Grinsekatze," sagte Alice:

"allow me to introduce it."
53.2

"Erlaube mir, sie vorzustellen."

"I don't like the look of it at all," said the King:
54.1

"Das gefällt mir gar nicht," sagte der König:

"however, it may kiss my hand if it likes."
54.2

"aber es darf mir die Hand küssen, wenn es will."

55.1 **"I'd rather not," the Cat remarked.**
"Lieber nicht," sagte die Katze.

56.1 **"Don't be impertinent," said the King,**
"Sei nicht unverschämt," sagte der König,

56.2 **"and don't look at me like that!"**
"und sieh mich nicht so an!"

56.3 **He got behind Alice as he spoke.**
Er stellte sich hinter Alice, während er sprach.

57.1 **"A cat may look at a king," said Alice.**
"Eine Katze darf einen König anschauen," sagte Alice.

57.2 **"I've read that in some book, but I don't remember where."**
"Das habe ich in irgendeinem Buch gelesen, aber ich weiß nicht mehr, wo."

58.1 **"Well, it must be removed,"**
"Nun, sie muss weg,"

58.2 **said the King very decidedly, and he called the Queen, who was passing at the moment:**
sagte der König sehr entschieden, und er rief die Königin, die gerade vorbeikam:

58.3 **"My dear!**
"Meine Liebe!

58.4 **I wish you would have this cat removed!"**
Ich wünschte, du würdest diese Katze entfernen lassen!"

The Queen had only one way of settling all difficulties, great or small. 59.1

Die Königin kannte nur einen Weg, um alle Schwierigkeiten, ob groß oder klein, zu lösen.

"Off with his head!" she said, without even looking round. 59.2

"Ab mit dem Kopf!" sagte sie, ohne sich umzusehen.

"I'll fetch the executioner myself," 60.1

"Ich werde den Henker selbst holen,"

said the King eagerly, and he hurried off. 60.2

sagte der König eifrig und eilte davon.

Alice thought she might as well go back, and see how the game was going on, as she heard the Queen's voice in the distance, screaming with passion. 61.1

Alice dachte, sie könnte auch zurückgehen und nachsehen, wie das Spiel weiterging, als sie in der Ferne die Stimme der Königin hörte, die vor Leidenschaft schrie.

She had already heard her sentence three of the players to be executed for having missed their turns, and she did not like the look of things at all, as the game was in such confusion that she never knew whether it was her turn or not. 61.2

Sie hatte bereits gehört, wie sie drei Spieler zur Hinrichtung verurteilte, weil sie ihren Zug verpasst hatten, und das gefiel ihr gar nicht, denn das Spiel war so verworren, dass sie nie wusste, ob sie an der Reihe war oder nicht.

So she went in search of her hedgehog. 61.3

Also ging sie auf die Suche nach ihrem Igel.

62.1 The hedgehog was engaged in a fight with another hedgehog, which seemed to Alice an excellent opportunity for croqueting one of them with the other:

Der Igel war in einen Kampf mit einem anderen Igel verwickelt, was Alice als eine ausgezeichnete Gelegenheit erschien, einen von ihnen mit dem anderen zu kreuzen:

62.2 the only difficulty was, that her flamingo was gone across to the other side of the garden, where Alice could see it trying in a helpless sort of way to fly up into a tree.

Das einzige Problem war, dass ihr Flamingo auf die andere Seite des Gartens gegangen war, wo Alice ihn sehen konnte, wie er hilflos versuchte, auf einen Baum zu fliegen.

63.1 By the time she had caught the flamingo and brought it back, the fight was over, and both the hedgehogs were out of sight:

Als sie den Flamingo gefangen und zurückgebracht hatte, war der Kampf vorbei, und die beiden Igel waren außer Sichtweite:

63.2 "but it doesn't matter much," thought Alice,

"Aber das macht nichts," dachte Alice,

63.3 "as all the arches are gone from this side of the ground."

"denn alle Bögen sind von dieser Seite des Bodens verschwunden."

63.4 So she tucked it away under her arm, that it might not escape again, and went back for a little more conversation with her friend.

Sie verstaute ihn unter ihrem Arm, damit er nicht wieder entkommen konnte, und ging zurück, um sich noch ein wenig mit ihrer Freundin zu unterhalten.

When she got back to the Cheshire Cat, she was surprised to find quite a large crowd collected round it:

64.1

Als sie zur Grinsekatze zurückkam, stellte sie zu ihrer Überraschung fest, dass sich eine große Menschenmenge um sie herum versammelt hatte:

there was a dispute going on between the executioner, the King, and the Queen, who were all talking at once, while all the rest were quite silent, and looked very uncomfortable.

64.2

Es gab einen Streit zwischen dem Henker, dem König und der Königin, die sich alle gleichzeitig unterhielten, während alle anderen ganz still waren und sehr unbehaglich aussahen.

The moment Alice appeared, she was appealed to by all three to settle the question, and they repeated their arguments to her, though, as they all spoke at once, she found it very hard indeed to make out exactly what they said.

65.1

In dem Moment, in dem Alice erschien, wurde sie von allen dreien aufgefordert, die Frage zu klären, und sie wiederholten ihr gegenüber ihre Argumente, obwohl es ihr, da sie alle gleichzeitig sprachen, sehr schwerfiel, genau zu verstehen, was sie sagten.

The executioner's argument was, that you couldn't cut off a head unless there was a body to cut it off from:

66.1

Das Argument des Scharfrichters war, dass man einen Kopf nicht abschlagen könne, wenn kein Körper vorhanden sei, von dem er abgetrennt werden könne:

66.2 that he had never had to do such a thing before, and he wasn't going to begin at his time of life.

Er habe so etwas noch nie tun müssen, und er werde auch nicht damit anfangen, wenn er noch am Leben sei.

67.1 The King's argument was, that anything that had a head could be beheaded, and that you weren't to talk nonsense.

Das Argument des Königs war, dass alles, was einen Kopf hat, geköpft werden kann, und dass man keinen Unsinn reden darf.

68.1 The Queen's argument was, that if something wasn't done about it in less than no time she'd have everybody executed, all round.

Das Argument der Königin war, dass sie, wenn nicht innerhalb kürzester Zeit etwas unternommen würde, alle hinrichten lassen würde, und zwar alle.

68.2 (It was this last remark that had made the whole party look so grave and anxious.)

(Es war diese letzte Bemerkung, die die ganze Gruppe so ernst und besorgt aussehen ließ.)

69.1 Alice could think of nothing else to say but "It belongs to the Duchess:

Alice fiel nichts anderes ein, als zu sagen:

69.2 you'd better ask her about it."

"Es gehört der Herzogin, du solltest sie danach fragen."

70.1 "She's in prison," the Queen said to the executioner:

"Sie ist im Gefängnis," sagte die Königin zum Henker:

"fetch her here." And the executioner went off like an arrow. 70.2

"Holt sie her." Und der Scharfrichter schoss wie ein Pfeil los.

The Cat's head began fading away the moment he was gone, and, by the time he had come back with the Duchess, it had entirely disappeared; 71.1

Der Kopf der Katze begann zu verschwinden, sobald er weg war, und als er mit der Herzogin zurückkam, war er ganz verschwunden;

so the King and the executioner ran wildly up and down looking for it, while the rest of the party went back to the game. 71.2

der König und der Scharfrichter liefen wild auf und ab, um ihn zu suchen, während der Rest der Gesellschaft zum Spiel zurückkehrte.

CHAPTER IX. The Mock Turtle's Story

KAPITEL IX. Die Geschichte der Spottschildkröte

1.1 "You can't think how glad I am to see you again, you dear old thing."

"Du kannst dir nicht vorstellen, wie froh ich bin, dich wiederzusehen, du liebes altes Ding."

1.2 said the Duchess, as she tucked her arm affectionately into Alice's, and they walked off together.

sagte die Herzogin, während sie ihren Arm liebevoll in den von Alice legte, und sie gingen gemeinsam davon.

2.1 Alice was very glad to find her in such a pleasant temper, and thought to herself that perhaps it was only the pepper that had made her so savage when they met in the kitchen.

Alice war sehr froh, sie so gut gelaunt vorzufinden, und dachte bei sich, dass es vielleicht nur der Pfeffer war, der sie so wild gemacht hatte, als sie sich in der Küche trafen.

"When I'm a Duchess," 3.1

"Wenn ich eine Herzogin bin,"

she said to herself, (not in a very hopeful tone 3.2
though),

sagte sie zu sich selbst (allerdings nicht in einem sehr
hoffnungsvollen Ton),

"I won't have any pepper in my kitchen at all. 3.3

"werde ich überhaupt keinen Pfeffer in meiner Küche
haben.

Soup does very well without — Maybe it's always 3.4
pepper that makes people hot- tempered,"

Vielleicht ist es immer der Pfeffer, der die Leute hitzig
macht,"

she went on, very much pleased at having found out a 3.5
new kind of rule,

fuhr sie fort, sehr erfreut darüber, eine neue Regel entdeckt
zu haben,

"and vinegar that makes them sour — and camomile 3.6
that makes them bitter — and — and barley-sugar
and such things that make children sweet-tempered.

"und der Essig, der sie sauer macht, und die Kamille, die sie
bitter macht, und der Gerstenzucker und solche Dinge, die
die Kinder süß machen.

I only wish people knew that: 3.7

Ich wünschte nur, die Leute wüssten das:

then they wouldn't be so stingy about it, you 3.8
know — "

dann wären sie nicht so geizig damit, weißt du — "

4.1 She had quite forgotten the Duchess by this time,

Sie hatte die Herzogin inzwischen ganz vergessen und war ein wenig erschrocken,

4.2 and was a little startled when she heard her voice close to her ear.

als sie ihre Stimme dicht an ihrem Ohr hörte.

4.3 "You're thinking about something, my dear, and that makes you forget to talk.

"Du denkst an etwas, meine Liebe, und das lässt dich vergessen zu sprechen.

4.4 I can't tell you just now what the moral of that is, but I shall remember it in a bit."

Ich kann dir jetzt noch nicht sagen, was die Moral davon ist, aber ich werde mich gleich daran erinnern."

5.1 "Perhaps it hasn't one," Alice ventured to remark.

"Vielleicht hat es keinen," wagte Alice zu bemerken.

6.1 "Tut, tut, child!" said the Duchess.

"Tut, tut, Kind!" sagte die Herzogin.

6.2 "Everything's got a moral, if only you can find it."

"Alles hat eine Moral, wenn man sie nur finden kann."

6.3 And she squeezed herself up closer to Alice's side as she spoke.

Und während sie sprach, drückte sie sich noch näher an Alice' Seite.

7.1 Alice did not much like keeping so close to her:

Alice mochte es nicht, so nahe bei ihr zu sein:

first, because the Duchess was very ugly; and 7.2
secondly, because she was exactly the right height
to rest her chin upon Alice's shoulder, and it was an
uncomfortably sharp chin.

erstens, weil die Herzogin sehr hässlich war, und zweitens,
weil sie genau die richtige Größe hatte, um ihr Kinn auf
Alices Schulter zu legen, und es war ein unangenehm
spitzes Kinn.

However, she did not like to be rude, so she bore it as 7.3
well as she could.

Aber sie wollte nicht unhöflich sein, also ertrug sie es, so
gut sie konnte.

"The game's going on rather better now," she said, 8.1

"Das Spiel läuft jetzt etwas besser," sagte sie,

by way of keeping up the conversation a little. 8.2

um die Unterhaltung ein wenig aufrechtzuerhalten.

"'Tis so," said the Duchess: 9.1

"So ist es," sagte die Herzogin, "und die Moral davon ist:

"and the moral of that is — 'Oh, 'tis love, 9.2

'Oh, 'tis love,

'tis love, that makes the world go round! "' 9.3

'tis love, that makes the world go round! "'

"Somebody said," Alice whispered, 10.1

"Jemand hat gesagt," flüsterte Alice,

10.2 "that it's done by everybody minding their own business!"

"dass das jeder macht, der sich um seinen eigenen Kram kümmert!"

11.1 "Ah, well!

"Ah, gut!

11.2 It means much the same thing," said the Duchess, digging her sharp little chin into Alice's shoulder as she added, "and the moral of that is — 'Take care of the sense, and the sounds will take care of themselves.'"

Es bedeutet so ziemlich das Gleiche," sagte die Herzogin und drückte ihr spitzes Kinn auf Alices Schulter, während sie hinzufügte, "und die Moral davon ist: 'Kümmere dich um den Sinn, und die Töne werden sich von selbst erledigen.'"

12.1 "How fond she is of finding morals in things!"

"Wie gern sie die Dinge moralisch bewertet!"

12.2 Alice thought to herself.

dachte Alice bei sich.

13.1 "I dare say you're wondering why I don't put my arm round your waist,"

"Sie fragen sich sicher, warum ich meinen Arm nicht um Ihre Taille lege,"

13.2 the Duchess said after a pause: "the reason is,

sagte die Herzogin nach einer Pause: "Der Grund ist,

13.3 that I'm doubtful about the temper of your flamingo.

dass ich an der Laune Ihres Flamingos zweifle.

Shall I try the experiment?"

13.4

Soll ich das Experiment wagen?"

"He might bite,"

14.1

"Er könnte beißen,"

Alice cautiously replied, not feeling at all anxious to have the experiment tried.

14.2

antwortete Alice vorsichtig, da sie keine Lust hatte, das Experiment zu wagen.

"Very true," said the Duchess:

15.1

"Sehr richtig," sagte die Herzogin:

"flamingoes and mustard both bite.

15.2

"Flamingos und Senf beißen beide.

And the moral of that is — 'Birds of a feather flock together."'

15.3

Und die Moral davon ist: 'Gleich und gleich gesellt sich gern."'

"Only mustard isn't a bird," Alice remarked.

16.1

"Nur Senf ist kein Vogel," bemerkte Alice.

"Right, as usual," said the Duchess:

17.1

"Richtig, wie immer," sagte die Herzogin:

"what a clear way you have of putting things!"

17.2

"wie klar Sie die Dinge formulieren!"

"It's a mineral, I think," said Alice.

18.1

"Ich glaube, es ist ein Mineral," sagte Alice.

19.1 "Of course it is,"
"Natürlich,"

19.2 said the Duchess, who seemed ready to agree to everything that Alice said;
sagte die Herzogin, die allem, was Alice sagte, zuzustimmen schien,

19.3 "there's a large mustard-mine near here.
"hier in der Nähe gibt es eine große Senfmine.

19.4 And the moral of that is — 'The more there is of mine,
Und die Moral von der Geschicht' ist: Je mehr es von mir gibt,

19.5 the less there is of yours. "'
desto weniger gibt es von dir. "'

20.1 "Oh, I know!"
"Oh, ich weiß!"

20.2 exclaimed Alice, who had not attended to this last remark,
rief Alice aus, die diese letzte Bemerkung nicht beachtet hatte,

20.3 "it's a vegetable. It doesn't look like one, but it is."
"es ist ein Gemüse. Es sieht nicht so aus, aber es ist eins."

21.1 "I quite agree with you," said the Duchess;
"Ich bin ganz Ihrer Meinung," sagte die Herzogin;

"and the moral of that is — 'Be what you would seem to be' — or if you'd like it put more simply — 'Never imagine yourself not to be otherwise than what it might appear to others that what you were or might have been was not otherwise than what you had been would have appeared to them to be otherwise.'"

21.2

"und die Moral davon ist: 'Sei, was du zu sein scheinst - oder, wenn Sie es einfacher ausdrücken wollen: 'Bilde dir nie ein, dass du nicht anders bist, als es anderen erscheinen mag, dass das, was du warst oder hättest sein können, nicht anders war, als das, was du gewesen bist, ihnen anders erschienen wäre.'"

"I think I should understand that better,"

22.1

"Ich glaube, ich würde es besser verstehen,"

Alice said very politely,

22.2

sagte Alice sehr höflich,

"if I had it written down: but I can't quite follow it as you say it."

22.3

"wenn ich es aufgeschrieben hätte, aber so wie du es sagst, kann ich es nicht ganz nachvollziehen."

"That's nothing to what I could say if I chose,"

23.1

"Das ist nichts im Vergleich zu dem, was ich sagen könnte, wenn ich wollte,"

the Duchess replied, in a pleased tone.

23.2

antwortete die Herzogin in einem zufriedenen Ton.

"Pray don't trouble yourself to say it any longer than that,"

24.1

"Mach dir bitte nicht die Mühe, es noch länger zu sagen,"

24.2 **said Alice.**
sagte Alice.

25.1 **"Oh, don't talk about trouble!" said the Duchess.**
"Oh, reden Sie nicht von Ärger!" sagte die Herzogin.

25.2 **"I make you a present of everything I've said as yet."**
"Ich schenke dir alles, was ich bis jetzt gesagt habe."

26.1 **"A cheap sort of present!" thought Alice.**
"Ein billiges Geschenk!" dachte Alice.

26.2 **"I'm glad they don't give birthday presents like that!"**
"Ich bin froh, dass es solche Geburtstagsgeschenke nicht gibt!"

26.3 **But she did not venture to say it out loud.**
Aber sie wagte es nicht, es laut auszusprechen.

27.1 **"Thinking again?"**
"Denkst du schon wieder?"

27.2 **the Duchess asked, with another dig of her sharp little chin.**
fragte die Herzogin mit einem weiteren Stoß ihres spitzen Kinns.

28.1 **"I've a right to think,"**
"Ich habe ein Recht zu denken,"

28.2 **said Alice sharply, for she was beginning to feel a little worried.**
sagte Alice scharf, denn sie begann, sich ein wenig Sorgen zu machen.

"Just about as much right," said the Duchess,   29.1
"Ungefähr so viel Recht," sagte die Herzogin,

"as pigs have to fly; and the m — "   29.2
"wie die Schweine zu fliegen haben; und die M — "

But here, to Alice's great surprise, the Duchess's voice   30.1
died away, even in the middle of her favourite word
Doch da erstarb zu Alices großer Überraschung die Stimme
der Herzogin, sogar mitten in ihrem Lieblingswort

'moral,'   30.2
"Moral,"

and the arm that was linked into hers began to   30.3
tremble.
und der Arm, der mit ihrem verbunden war, begann zu
zittern.

Alice looked up, and there stood the Queen in front   30.4
of them, with her arms folded, frowning like a
thunderstorm.
Alice blickte auf, und vor ihnen stand die Königin mit
verschränkten Armen, die Stirn runzelnd wie ein Gewitter.

"A fine day, your Majesty!"   31.1
"Ein schöner Tag, Eure Majestät!"

the Duchess began in a low, weak voice.   31.2
begann die Herzogin mit leiser, schwacher Stimme.

"Now, I give you fair warning,"   32.1
"Ich warne dich,"

32.2 shouted the Queen, stamping on the ground as she spoke;

rief die Königin und stampfte auf den Boden, während sie sprach,

32.3 "either you or your head must be off,

"entweder du wirst geköpft oder du wirst geköpft,

32.4 and that in about half no time! Take your choice!"

und zwar in kürzester Zeit! Du hast die Wahl!"

33.1 The Duchess took her choice, and was gone in a moment.

Die Herzogin traf ihre Wahl und war im Nu verschwunden.

34.1 "Let's go on with the game,"

"Lass uns weiterspielen,"

34.2 the Queen said to Alice; and Alice was too much frightened to say a word, but slowly followed her back to the croquet-ground.

sagte die Königin zu Alice, und Alice war zu sehr erschrocken, um ein Wort zu sagen, sondern folgte ihr langsam zurück zum Krocketplatz.

35.1 The other guests had taken advantage of the Queen's absence, and were resting in the shade: however, the moment they saw her, they hurried back to the game, the Queen merely remarking that a moment's delay would cost them their lives.

Die anderen Gäste hatten die Abwesenheit der Königin ausgenutzt und ruhten sich im Schatten aus; sobald sie sie jedoch sahen, eilten sie zum Spiel zurück, wobei die Königin lediglich anmerkte, dass ein Moment der Verzögerung sie das Leben kosten würde.

All the time they were playing the Queen never left off quarrelling with the other players,

36.1

Während des ganzen Spiels hörte die Königin nicht auf,

and shouting:

36.2

mit den anderen Spielern zu streiten und zu schreien:

"Off with his head!" or "Off with her head!"

36.3

"Ab mit seinem Kopf!" oder "Ab mit ihrem Kopf!"

Those whom she sentenced were taken into custody by the soldiers, who of course had to leave off being arches to do this, so that by the end of half an hour or so there were no arches left, and all the players, except the King, the Queen, and Alice, were in custody and under sentence of execution.

36.4

Diejenigen, die sie verurteilte, wurden von den Soldaten in Gewahrsam genommen, die dafür natürlich nicht mehr Bogenschützen sein durften, so dass am Ende einer halben Stunde oder so keine Bogenschützen mehr übrig waren und alle Spieler, außer dem König, der Königin und Alice, in Gewahrsam und zur Hinrichtung verurteilt waren.

Then the Queen left off, quite out of breath, and said to Alice:

37.1

Dann ging die Königin ganz außer Atem weg und sagte zu Alice:

"Have you seen the Mock Turtle yet?"

37.2

"Hast du die Spottschildkröte schon gesehen?"

"No," said Alice.

38.1

"Nein," sagte Alice.

"I don't even know what a Mock Turtle is."

38.2

"Ich weiß nicht einmal, was eine Mock Turtle ist."

39.1 "It's the thing Mock Turtle Soup is made from," said the Queen.

"Daraus wird die Schildkrötensuppe gemacht," sagte die Königin.

40.1 "I never saw one, or heard of one,"

"Ich habe noch nie einen gesehen oder von einem gehört,"

40.2 said Alice.

sagte Alice.

41.1 "Come on, then," said the Queen,

"Dann komm," sagte die Königin,

41.2 "and he shall tell you his history,"

"und er wird dir seine Geschichte erzählen,"

42.1 As they walked off together, Alice heard the King say in a low voice, to the company generally:

Als sie zusammen gingen, hörte Alice, wie der König mit leiser Stimme zu allen Anwesenden sagte:

42.2 "You are all pardoned."

"Ihr seid alle begnadigt."

42.3 "Come, that's a good thing!"

"Das ist doch gut!"

42.4 she said to herself, for she had felt quite unhappy at the number of executions the Queen had ordered.

sagte sie zu sich selbst, denn sie war sehr unglücklich über die Anzahl der Hinrichtungen, die die Königin angeordnet hatte.

They very soon came upon a Gryphon, 43.1

Schon bald stießen sie auf einen Greifen,

lying fast asleep in the sun. 43.2

der in der Sonne schlief.

(If you don't know what a Gryphon is, look at the 43.3
picture.)

(Wenn du nicht weißt, was ein Greif ist, sieh dir das Bild
an.)

"Up, lazy thing!" said the Queen, 43.4

"Steh auf, du Faulpelz!" sagte die Königin,

"and take this young lady to see the Mock Turtle, 43.5

"und führe die junge Dame zur Spottschildkröte,

and to hear his history. 43.6

um ihre Geschichte zu hören.

I must go back and see after some executions I have 43.7
ordered;"

Ich muss zurückgehen und mich um einige von mir
angeordnete Hinrichtungen kümmern,"

and she walked off, leaving Alice alone with the 43.8
Gryphon.

und sie ging weg und ließ Alice mit dem Greifen allein.

Alice did not quite like the look of the creature, but 43.9
on the whole she thought it would be quite as safe to
stay with it as to go after that savage Queen: so she
waited.

Alice gefiel das Aussehen des Tieres nicht besonders,
aber im Großen und Ganzen hielt sie es für genauso
sicher, bei ihm zu bleiben, wie dieser wilden Königin
hinterherzujagen, und so wartete sie.

44.1 The Gryphon sat up and rubbed its eyes: then it watched the Queen till she was out of sight: then it chuckled.

Der Greif setzte sich auf und rieb sich die Augen; dann sah er der Königin nach, bis sie außer Sichtweite war; dann kicherte er.

44.2 "What fun!"

"Was für ein Spaß!"

44.3 said the Gryphon, half to itself, half to Alice.

sagte der Greif, halb zu sich selbst, halb zu Alice.

45.1 "What is the fun?" said Alice.

"Was ist daran so lustig?" fragte Alice.

46.1 "Why, she," said the Gryphon. "It's all her fancy, that:

"Ja, sie," sagte der Greif. "Das ist nur ihre Einbildung:

46.2 they never executes nobody, you know. Come on!"

Sie richten niemanden hin, weißt du. Komm mit!"

47.1 "Everybody says 'come on!' here," thought Alice,

"Sagen alle 'Komm schon!' hier," dachte Alice,

47.2 as she went slowly after it:

als sie langsam hinterherging:

47.3 "I never was so ordered about in all my life,

"Ich bin in meinem ganzen Leben noch nie so herumkommandiert worden,

47.4 never!"

niemals!"

They had not gone far before they saw the Mock Turtle in the distance, sitting sad and lonely on a little ledge of rock, and, as they came nearer, Alice could hear him sighing as if his heart would break. 48.1

Sie waren noch nicht weit gegangen, als sie in der Ferne die Mock Turtle sahen, die traurig und einsam auf einem kleinen Felsvorsprung saß, und als sie näher kamen, konnte Alice ihn seufzen hören, als würde sein Herz brechen.

She pitied him deeply. "What is his sorrow?" 48.2

Sie hatte großes Mitleid mit ihm. "Was ist sein Kummer?"

she asked the Gryphon, and the Gryphon answered, very nearly in the same words as before, 48.3

fragte sie den Greif, und der Greif antwortete, fast mit denselben Worten wie zuvor:

"It's all his fancy, that: he hasn't got no sorrow, you know. 48.4

"Das bildet er sich nur ein: Er hat keinen Kummer, weißt du.

Come on!" 48.5

Komm schon!"

So they went up to the Mock Turtle, who looked at them with large eyes full of tears, but said nothing. 49.1

So gingen sie zu der falschen Schildkröte, die sie mit großen, tränenüberströmten Augen ansah, aber nichts sagte.

"This here young lady," said the Gryphon, 50.1

"Diese junge Dame hier," sagte der Greif,

"she wants for to know your history, she do." 50.2

"sie will deine Geschichte wissen."

51.1 "I'll tell it her,"
"Ich werde es ihr erzählen,"

51.2 said the Mock Turtle in a deep, hollow tone:
sagte die Spottschildkröte in einem tiefen, hohlen Ton:

51.3 "sit down, both of you, and don't speak a word till I've finished."
"Setzt euch beide hin und sprecht kein Wort, bis ich fertig bin."

52.1 So they sat down,
Sie setzten sich also hin,

52.2 and nobody spoke for some minutes.
und einige Minuten lang sagte niemand etwas.

52.3 Alice thought to herself,
Alice dachte bei sich:

52.4 "I don't see how he can ever finish, if he doesn't begin."
"Ich weiß nicht, wie er jemals fertig werden kann, wenn er nicht anfängt."

52.5 But she waited patiently.
Aber sie wartete geduldig.

53.1 "Once,"
"Einst,"

53.2 said the Mock Turtle at last, with a deep sigh,
sagte die falsche Schildkröte schließlich mit einem tiefen Seufzer,

"I was a real Turtle." 53.3
"war ich eine echte Schildkröte."

These words were followed by a very long silence, 54.1
Auf diese Worte folgte ein sehr langes Schweigen,

broken only by an occasional exclamation of 54.2
"Hjckrrh!"
das nur durch ein gelegentliches "Hjckrrh!"

from the Gryphon, 54.3
des Greifen und das ständige,

and the constant heavy sobbing of the Mock Turtle. 54.4
heftige Schluchzen der Mock Turtle unterbrochen wurde.

Alice was very nearly getting up and saying: 54.5
Fast wäre Alice aufgestanden und hätte gesagt:

"Thank you, sir, for your interesting story," 54.6
"Vielen Dank, Sir, für Ihre interessante Geschichte,"

but she could not help thinking there must be more 54.7
to come, so she sat still and said nothing.
aber sie konnte nicht anders, als zu denken, dass noch
mehr kommen musste, also blieb sie sitzen und sagte
nichts.

"When we were little," 55.1
"Als wir klein waren,"

the Mock Turtle went on at last, more calmly, though 55.2
still sobbing a little now and then,
fuhr die Mock Turtle schließlich etwas ruhiger fort,
obwohl sie immer noch ab und zu schluchzte,

55.3 **"we went to school in the sea.**
"gingen wir im Meer zur Schule.

55.4 **The master was an old Turtle -**
Der Lehrer war eine alte Schildkröte -

55.5 **we used to call him Tortoise -"**
wir nannten ihn Tortoise -"

56.1 **"Why did you call him Tortoise, if he wasn't one?"**
"Warum hast du ihn Schildkröte genannt, wenn er keine war?"

56.2 **Alice asked.**
fragte Alice.

57.1 **"We called him Tortoise because he taught us,"**
"Wir haben ihn Schildkröte genannt, weil er uns gelehrt hat,"

57.2 **said the Mock Turtle angrily:**
sagte die Spottschildkröte wütend:

57.3 **"really you are very dull!"**
"Ihr seid wirklich sehr dumm!"

58.1 **"You ought to be ashamed of yourself for asking such a simple question,"**
"Du solltest dich schämen, eine so einfache Frage zu stellen,"

added the Gryphon; and then they both sat silent and looked at poor Alice, who felt ready to sink into the earth.

58.2

fügte der Greif hinzu, und dann saßen sie beide schweigend da und sahen die arme Alice an, die das Gefühl hatte, in der Erde zu versinken.

At last the Gryphon said to the Mock Turtle, "Drive on,

58.3

Schließlich sagte der Greif zu der Spottschildkröte: "Fahr los,

old fellow! Don't be all day about it!"

58.4

alter Freund! Mach nicht den ganzen Tag darüber her!"

and he went on in these words:

58.5

und er fuhr mit diesen Worten fort:

"Yes, we went to school in the sea, though you mayn't believe it — "

59.1

"Ja, wir sind im Meer zur Schule gegangen, auch wenn du es nicht glauben magst — "

"I never said I didn't!"

60.1

"Ich habe nie gesagt, dass ich das nicht will!"

interrupted Alice.

60.2

unterbrach Alice.

"You did," said the Mock Turtle.

61.1

"Das hast du," sagte die Scheinschildkröte.

"Hold your tongue!" added the Gryphon,

62.1

"Hüte deine Zunge!" fügte der Greif hinzu,

62.2 **before Alice could speak again.**
bevor Alice wieder sprechen konnte.

62.3 **The Mock Turtle went on.**
Die Pseudo-Schildkröte fuhr fort.

63.1 **"We had the best of educations — in fact, we went to school every day — "**
"Wir hatten die beste Ausbildung - wir gingen jeden Tag zur Schule — "

64.1 **"I've been to a day-school, too," said Alice;**
"Ich war auch in einer Tagesschule," sagte Alice,

64.2 **"you needn't be so proud as all that."**
"du brauchst nicht so stolz zu sein."

65.1 **"With extras?" asked the Mock Turtle a little anxiously.**
"Mit Extras?" fragte die Mock Turtle ein wenig ängstlich.

66.1 **"Yes," said Alice,**
"Ja," sagte Alice,

66.2 **"we learned French and music."**
"wir haben Französisch und Musik gelernt."

67.1 **"And washing?" said the Mock Turtle.**
"Und waschen?" fragte die falsche Schildkröte.

68.1 **"Certainly not!" said Alice indignantly.**
"Natürlich nicht!" sagte Alice entrüstet.

"Ah! then yours wasn't a really good school," 69.1
"Ah! Dann war eure Schule nicht wirklich gut,"

said the Mock Turtle in a tone of great relief. 69.2
sagte die Mock Turtle in einem Ton großer Erleichterung.

"Now at ours they had at the end of the bill: 69.3
"Bei uns hieß es am Ende der Rechnung:

'French, music, and washing — extra. "' 69.4
'Französisch, Musik und Waschen extra'."

"You couldn't have wanted it much," said Alice; 70.1
"Du konntest es gar nicht wollen," sagte Alice,

"living at the bottom of the sea." 70.2
"auf dem Meeresgrund zu leben."

"I couldn't afford to learn it." 71.1
"Ich konnte es mir nicht leisten, es zu lernen."

said the Mock Turtle with a sigh. 71.2
sagte die Mock Turtle mit einem Seufzer.

"I only took the regular course." 71.3
"Ich habe nur den normalen Kurs belegt."

"What was that?" inquired Alice. 72.1
"Was war das?" erkundigte sich Alice.

"Reeling and Writhing, of course, to begin with," 73.1
"Taumelnd und sich windend natürlich zuerst,"

the Mock Turtle replied; 73.2
antwortete die falsche Schildkröte,

73.3 "and then the different branches of Arithmetic -
"und dann die verschiedenen Zweige der Arithmetik -

73.4 Ambition, Distraction, Uglification, and Derision."
Bestürzung, Ablenkung, Verblüffung und Spott."

74.1 "I never heard of 'Uglification, "'
"Ich habe noch nie von 'Uglification' gehört,"

74.2 Alice ventured to say. "What is it?"
wagte Alice zu sagen. "Was ist das?"

75.1 The Gryphon lifted up both its paws in surprise.
"What!
Der Greif hob überrascht seine beiden Pfoten. "Was!

75.2 Never heard of uglifying!" it exclaimed.
Ich habe noch nie etwas von Verschönerung gehört!" rief er
aus.

75.3 "You know what to beautify is, I suppose?"
"Du weißt wohl, was verschönern ist?"

76.1 "Yes," said Alice doubtfully:
"Ja," sagte Alice zweifelnd:

76.2 "it means — to — make — anything — prettier."
"Es bedeutet, irgendetwas zu verschönern."

77.1 "Well, then," the Gryphon went on,
"Nun denn," fuhr der Greif fort,

"if you don't know what to uglify is, you are a simpleton."

77.2

"wenn du nicht weißt, was hässlich sein bedeutet, bist du ein Einfaltspinsel."

Alice did not feel encouraged to ask any more questions about it, so she turned to the Mock Turtle, and said:

78.1

Alice fühlte sich nicht ermutigt, weitere Fragen zu stellen, also wandte sie sich an die falsche Schildkröte und sagte:

"What else had you to learn?"

78.2

"Was musstest du noch lernen?"

"Well, there was Mystery,"

79.1

"Nun, es gab Mystery,"

the Mock Turtle replied, counting off the subjects on his flappers,

79.2

antwortete die Mock Turtle und zählte die Fächer auf seinen Klappen auf,

" — Mystery, ancient and modern, with Seaography:

79.3

"Mystery, ancient and modern, with Seaography:

then Drawling — the Drawling-master was an old conger-eel,

79.4

then Drawling-the Drawling-master was a old conger-eel,

that used to come once a week:

79.5

that used to come once a week:

he taught us Drawling, Stretching, and Fainting in Coils."

79.6

he taught us Drawling, Stretching, and Overting in Coils."

80.1 "What was that like?" said Alice.
"Wie war das?" fragte Alice.

81.1 "Well, I can't show it you myself,"
"Nun, ich kann es dir nicht selbst zeigen,"

81.2 the Mock Turtle said: "I'm too stiff.
sagte die falsche Schildkröte: "Ich bin zu steif.

81.3 And the Gryphon never learnt it."
Und der Greif hat es nie gelernt."

82.1 "Hadn't time," said the Gryphon:
"Ich hatte keine Zeit," sagte der Greif:

82.2 "I went to the Classics master, though.
"Ich bin aber zum Meister der Klassiker gegangen.

82.3 He was an old crab, he was."
Er war ein alter Kauz."

83.1 "I never went to him," the Mock Turtle said with a sigh:
"Ich bin nie zu ihm gegangen," sagte die Mock Turtle seufzend:

83.2 "he taught Laughing and Grief, they used to say."
"Er lehrte das Lachen und den Kummer, hieß es früher."

84.1 "So he did, so he did," said the Gryphon,
"Das hat er, das hat er," seufzte der Greif seinerseits,

84.2 sighing in his turn; and both creatures hid their faces in their paws.
und beide Tiere verbargen ihr Gesicht in den Pfoten.

"And how many hours a day did you do lessons?" 85.1
"Und wie viele Stunden am Tag hast du Unterricht?"

said Alice, in a hurry to change the subject. 85.2
fragte Alice, um das Thema zu wechseln.

"Ten hours the first day," said the Mock Turtle: 86.1
"Zehn Stunden am ersten Tag," sagte die falsche
Schildkröte:

"nine the next, and so on." 86.2
"Am nächsten Tag neun und so weiter."

"What a curious plan!" exclaimed Alice. 87.1
"Was für ein merkwürdiger Plan!" rief Alice aus.

"That's the reason they're called lessons," 88.1
"Das ist der Grund, warum man sie Lektionen nennt,"

the Gryphon remarked: 88.2
bemerkte der Greifen:

"because they lessen from day to day." 88.3
"Weil sie von Tag zu Tag weniger werden."

This was quite a new idea to Alice, and she thought it 89.1
over a little before she made her next remark.
Das war eine ganz neue Idee für Alice, und sie dachte ein
wenig darüber nach, bevor sie ihre nächste Bemerkung
machte.

"Then the eleventh day must have been a holiday?" 89.2
"Dann muss der elfte Tag ein Feiertag gewesen sein?"

90.1 **"Of course it was," said the Mock Turtle.**
"Natürlich war es das," sagte die Scheinschildkröte.

91.1 **"And how did you manage on the twelfth?"**
"Und wie ist es dir am zwölften Tag ergangen?"

91.2 **Alice went on eagerly.**
fuhr Alice eifrig fort.

92.1 **"That's enough about lessons,"**
"Genug von den Lektionen,"

92.2 **the Gryphon interrupted in a very decided tone:**
unterbrach der Greif in einem sehr entschiedenen Ton:

92.3 **"tell her something about the games now."**
"Erzähle ihr jetzt etwas über die Spiele."

CHAPTER X. The Lobster Quadrille

KAPITEL X. Die Hummerquadrille

1.1 The Mock Turtle sighed deeply, and drew the back of one flapper across his eyes.

Die Mock Turtle seufzte tief und strich sich mit dem Rücken einer Klappe über die Augen.

1.2 He looked at Alice, and tried to speak, but for a minute or two sobs choked his voice.

Er sah Alice an und versuchte zu sprechen, aber ein oder zwei Minuten lang erstickten Schluchzer seine Stimme.

1.3 "Same as if he had a bone in his throat,"

"Als ob er einen Knochen im Hals hätte,"

1.4 said the Gryphon: and it set to work shaking him and punching him in the back.

sagte der Greif, schüttelte ihn und schlug ihm auf den Rücken.

1.5 At last the Mock Turtle recovered his voice, and, with tears running down his cheeks, he went on again: — .

Endlich erlangte die Spottschildkröte ihre Stimme wieder, und mit Tränen auf den Wangen fuhr sie fort.

"You may not have lived much under the sea -"   2.1
"Du hast vielleicht noch nicht viel unter dem Meer gelebt -"

("I haven't," said Alice) -   2.2
("Nein, habe ich nicht," sagte Alice) -

"and perhaps you were never even introduced to a   2.3
lobster -"
"und vielleicht hast du noch nie einen Hummer gesehen -"

(Alice began to say "I once tasted -"   2.4
(Alice begann zu sagen: "Ich habe ihn einmal gekostet -"

but checked herself hastily, and said "No, never")   2.5
aber sie zügelte sich, und sagte "Nein, nie")

"- so you can have no idea what a delightful thing a   2.6
Lobster Quadrille is!"
"- also kannst du dir nicht vorstellen, was für eine köstliche
Sache eine Hummerquadrille ist!"

"No, indeed," said Alice. "What sort of a dance is it?"   3.1
"Nein, wirklich," sagte Alice. "Was ist das für ein Tanz?"

"Why," said the Gryphon,   4.1
"Nun," sagte der Greif,

"you first form into a line along the sea- shore — "   4.2
"ihr bildet zuerst eine Reihe entlang des Meeresufers ..."

"Two lines!" cried the Mock Turtle.   5.1
"Zwei Leinen!" rief die Mock Turtle.

"Seals, turtles, salmon, and so on; then,   5.2
"Robben, Schildkröten, Lachse und so weiter; dann,

5.3 when you've cleared all the jelly-fish out of the way — "

wenn du alle Quallen aus dem Weg geräumt hast ..."

6.1 "That generally takes some time," interrupted the Gryphon.

"Das dauert in der Regel eine Weile," unterbrach der Greif.

7.1 " — you advance twice — "

" — du schießt zweimal vor — "

8.1 "Each with a lobster as a partner!" cried the Gryphon.

"Jeder mit einem Hummer als Partner!" rief der Greif.

9.1 "Of course," the Mock Turtle said: "advance twice,

"Natürlich," sagte die Mock Turtle: "Zweimal vorrücken,

9.2 set to partners — "

auf Partner einstellen — "

10.1 " — change lobsters, and retire in same order,"

"Hummer austauschen und sich in der gleichen Reihenfolge zurückziehen,"

10.2 continued the Gryphon.

fuhr der Greifen fort.

11.1 "Then, you know," the Mock Turtle went on,

"Dann, weißt du," fuhr die falsche Schildkröte fort,

11.2 "you throw the — "

"wirfst du die — "

"The lobsters!" shouted the Gryphon, with a bound into the air.

12.1

"Die Hummer!" rief der Greif mit einem Sprung in die Luft.

" — as far out to sea as you can — "

13.1

" — so weit wie möglich hinaus aufs Meer — "

"Swim after them!" screamed the Gryphon.

14.1

"Schwimmt hinterher!" schrie der Greif.

"Turn a somersault in the sea!"

15.1

"Mach einen Purzelbaum im Meer!"

cried the Mock Turtle, capering wildly about.

15.2

rief die falsche Schildkröte und hüpfte wild herum.

"Change lobsters again!"

16.1

"Wieder Hummer austauschen!"

yelled the Gryphon at the top of its voice.

16.2

schrie der Greif lauthals.

"Back to land again, and that's all the first figure,"

17.1

"Wieder zurück an Land, und das ist alles, was die erste Figur ausmacht,"

said the Mock Turtle, suddenly dropping his voice; and the two creatures, who had been jumping about like mad things all this time, sat down again very sadly and quietly, and looked at Alice.

17.2

sagte die falsche Schildkröte und senkte plötzlich ihre Stimme, und die beiden Wesen, die die ganze Zeit wie verrückt herumgesprungen waren, setzten sich wieder ganz traurig und ruhig hin und sahen Alice an.

18.1 "It must be a very pretty dance," said Alice timidly.
"Es muss ein sehr schöner Tanz sein," sagte Alice zaghaft.

19.1 "Would you like to see a little of it?"
"Möchtest du etwas davon sehen?"

19.2 said the Mock Turtle.
fragte die falsche Schildkröte.

20.1 "Very much indeed," said Alice.
"Sehr sogar," sagte Alice.

21.1 "Come, let's try the first figure!"
"Komm, lass uns die erste Figur ausprobieren!"

21.2 said the Mock Turtle to the Gryphon.
sagte die Scheinschildkröte zum Greifen.

21.3 "We can do without lobsters, you know.
"Wir können auch ohne Hummer auskommen, weißt du.

21.4 Which shall sing?"
Wer soll singen?"

22.1 "Oh, you sing," said the Gryphon.
"Oh, du singst," sagte der Greif.

22.2 "I've forgotten the words."
"Ich habe den Text vergessen."

So they began solemnly dancing round and round   23.1
Alice, every now and then treading on her toes when
they passed too close, and waving their forepaws to
mark the time, while the Mock Turtle sang this, very
slowly and sadly:-

So begannen sie feierlich um Alice herumzutanzen,
traten ihr ab und zu auf die Zehen, wenn sie ihr zu nahe
kamen, und winkten mit den Vorderpfoten, um die Zeit zu
markieren, während die Spottschildkröte ganz langsam
und traurig Folgendes sang:-

"Will you walk a little faster?"

"Kannst du ein bisschen schneller laufen?"

said a whiting to a snail.

sagte ein Weißling zu einer Schnecke.

"There's a porpoise close behind us,

"Ein Schweinswal ist dicht hinter uns,

and he's treading on my tail.

und er tritt mir auf den Schwanz.

See how eagerly the lobsters and the turtles all advance!

Seht, wie eifrig die Hummer und die Schildkröten voranschreiten!

They are waiting on the shingle -

Sie warten auf der Schindel -

will you come and join the dance?

kommst du und tanzt mit?

Will you, won't you, will you, won't you, will you join the dance?

Willst du, willst du nicht, willst du, willst du nicht, willst du den Tanz mitmachen?

230

Will you, won't you, will you, won't you, won't you join the dance?	Willst du, willst du nicht, willst du, willst du nicht, willst du nicht tanzen?
"You can really have no notion how delightful it will be	"Sie können sich gar nicht vorstellen, wie schön es sein wird
When they take us up and throw us, with the lobsters, out to sea!"	Wenn sie uns hochnehmen und mit den Hummern aufs Meer hinauswerfen!"
But the snail replied "Too far, too far!"	Aber die Schnecke antwortete: "Zu weit, zu weit!"
and gave a look askance — .	und warf einen fragenden Blick.
Said he thanked the whiting kindly,	Er bedankte sich höflich bei dem Weißen,
but he would not join the dance.	wollte aber nicht mit ihm tanzen.
Would not, could not, would not, could not, would not join the dance.	Wollte nicht, konnte nicht, wollte nicht, konnte nicht, wollte nicht mittanzen.
Would not, could not, would not, could not, could not join the dance.	Wollte nicht, konnte nicht, wollte nicht, konnte nicht, konnte nicht mittanzen.

"What matters it how far
we go?"

"Was spielt es für eine
Rolle, wie weit wir
gehen?"

his scaly friend replied.

antwortete sein
schuppiger Freund.

"There is another shore, you
know, upon the other side.

"Es gibt ein anderes
Ufer, weißt du, auf der
anderen Seite.

The further off from
England the nearer is to
France — .

Je weiter man sich von
England entfernt, desto
näher kommt man
Frankreich.

Then turn not pale, beloved
snail, but come and join the
dance.

Dann werde nicht blass,
geliebte Schnecke,
sondern komm und
tanze mit.

Will you, won't you, will
you, won't you, will you
join the dance?

Willst du, willst du
nicht, willst du, willst du
nicht, willst du den Tanz
mitmachen?

Will you, won't you, will
you, won't you, won't you
join the dance?"

Willst du, willst du nicht,
willst du, willst du nicht,
willst du nicht tanzen?"

"Thank you, it's a very interesting dance to watch," 25.1
"Danke, es ist ein sehr interessanter Tanz,"

said Alice, feeling very glad that it was over at last: 25.2
sagte Alice und war froh, dass er endlich vorbei war:

25.3 "and I do so like that curious song about the whiting!"

"Und ich mag dieses merkwürdige Lied über den Wittling sehr!"

26.1 "Oh, as to the whiting," said the Mock Turtle,

"Oh, was die Wittlinge angeht," sagte die Spottschildkröte,

26.2 "they — you've seen them, of course?"

"die hast du doch sicher gesehen?"

27.1 "Yes," said Alice, "I've often seen them at dinn — "

"Ja," sagte Alice, "ich habe sie oft beim Essen gesehen — ,"

27.2 she checked herself hastily.

sie zügelte sich schnell.

28.1 "I don't know where Dinn may be," said the Mock Turtle,

"Ich weiß nicht, wo Dinn sein mag," sagte die Mock Turtle,

28.2 "but if you've seen them so often, of course you know what they're like."

"aber wenn du sie so oft gesehen hast, weißt du natürlich, wie sie sind."

29.1 "I believe so," Alice replied thoughtfully.

"Ich glaube schon," antwortete Alice nachdenklich.

29.2 "They have their tails in their mouths -

"Sie haben ihre Schwänze im Maul -

29.3 and they're all over crumbs."

und sie stürzen sich auf die Krümel."

"You're wrong about the crumbs," said the Mock Turtle:

30.1

"Du irrst dich mit den Krümeln," sagte die falsche Schildkröte:

"crumbs would all wash off in the sea.

30.2

"Die Krümel würden alle im Meer abgewaschen werden.

But they have their tails in their mouths; and the reason is — "

30.3

Aber sie haben ihre Schwänze im Mund, und der Grund dafür ist — "

here the Mock Turtle yawned and shut his eyes.

30.4

Hier gähnte die Spottschildkröte und schloss die Augen.

— "Tell her about the reason and all that,"

30.5

— "Erzähl ihr den Grund dafür und all das,"

he said to the Gryphon.

30.6

sagte er zum Greif.

"The reason is," said the Gryphon,

31.1

"Der Grund ist," sagte der Greif,

"that they would go with the lobsters to the dance.

31.2

"dass sie mit den Hummern zum Tanz gehen wollten.

So they got thrown out to sea.

31.3

So wurden sie auf das Meer hinausgeworfen.

So they had to fall a long way.

31.4

So mussten sie einen langen Weg zurücklegen.

So they got their tails fast in their mouths.

31.5

So hatten sie ihre Schwänze fest im Maul.

31.6 So they couldn't get them out again. That's all."

So konnten sie sie nicht wieder herausholen. Das ist alles."

32.1 "Thank you," said Alice, "it's very interesting.

"Danke," sagte Alice, "das ist sehr interessant.

32.2 I never knew so much about a whiting before."

Ich wusste noch nie so viel über einen Wittling."

33.1 "I can tell you more than that, if you like,"

"Ich kann dir noch mehr sagen, wenn du willst,"

33.2 said the Gryphon. "Do you know why it's called a whiting?"

sagte der Greif. "Weißt du, warum man ihn Wittling nennt?"

34.1 "I never thought about it," said Alice. "Why?"

"Ich habe nie darüber nachgedacht," sagte Alice. "Warum?"

35.1 "It does the boots and shoes,"

"Es sind die Stiefel und Schuhe,"

35.2 the Gryphon replied very solemnly.

antwortete der Greif sehr feierlich.

36.1 Alice was thoroughly puzzled. "Does the boots and shoes!"

Alice war völlig verwirrt. "Hat die Stiefel und Schuhe!"

36.2 she repeated in a wondering tone.

wiederholte sie in einem verwunderten Ton.

"Why, what are your shoes done with?" said the
Gryphon.

37.1

"Womit sind denn deine Schuhe gemacht?" fragte der
Greif.

"I mean, what makes them so shiny?"

37.2

"Ich meine, warum glänzen sie so?"

Alice looked down at them,

38.1

Alice schaute auf sie hinunter und überlegte ein wenig,

and considered a little before she gave her answer.

38.2

bevor sie antwortete.

"They're done with blacking, I believe."

38.3

"Sie sind fertig mit dem Schwärzen, glaube ich."

"Boots and shoes under the sea,"

39.1

"Stiefel und Schuhe unter dem Meer,"

the Gryphon went on in a deep voice,

39.2

fuhr der Greif mit tiefer Stimme fort,

"are done with a whiting. Now you know."

39.3

"werden mit einem Wittling gemacht. Jetzt weißt du es."

"And what are they made of?"

40.1

"Und woraus sind sie gemacht?"

Alice asked in a tone of great curiosity.

40.2

fragte Alice in einem Ton großer Neugier.

"Soles and eels, of course,"

41.1

"Sohlen und Aale, natürlich,"

41.2 **the Gryphon replied rather impatiently:**
antwortete der Greif etwas ungeduldig:

41.3 **"any shrimp could have told you that."**
"Das hätte dir jede Garnele sagen können."

42.1 **"If I'd been the whiting," said Alice, whose thoughts were still running on the song, "I'd have said to the porpoise, 'Keep back, please:**
"Wenn ich der Weißfisch gewesen wäre," sagte Alice, deren Gedanken immer noch bei dem Lied waren, "hätte ich zu dem Tümmler gesagt:

42.2 **we don't want you with us! "'**
'Bleib bitte zurück, wir wollen dich nicht bei uns haben! "'

43.1 **"They were obliged to have him with them,"**
"Sie mussten ihn bei sich haben,"

43.2 **the Mock Turtle said:**
sagte die Spottschildkröte:

43.3 **"no wise fish would go anywhere without a porpoise."**
"Kein kluger Fisch würde ohne einen Schweinswal irgendwohin gehen."

44.1 **"Wouldn't it really?" said Alice in a tone of great surprise.**
"Wirklich nicht?" sagte Alice mit großer Überraschung.

45.1 **"Of course not," said the Mock Turtle:**
"Natürlich nicht," sagte die Spottschildkröte:

"why, if a fish came to me, and told me he was going a journey, I should say: 45.2
"Wenn ein Fisch zu mir käme und mir sagte, er gehe auf eine Reise, würde ich sagen:

'With what porpoise? "'   45.3
'Mit welchem Tümmler? "'

"Don't you mean 'purpose'?" said Alice.   46.1
"Meinst du nicht 'Zweck'?" fragte Alice.

"I mean what I say,"   47.1
"Ich meine, was ich sage,"

the Mock Turtle replied in an offended tone.   47.2
erwiderte die Spottschildkröte in beleidigtem Ton.

And the Gryphon added "Come,   47.3
Und der Greif fügte hinzu: "Komm,

let's hear some of your adventures."   47.4
lass uns von deinen Abenteuern hören."

"I could tell you my adventures -   48.1
"Ich könnte dir meine Abenteuer erzählen -

beginning from this morning,"   48.2
beginnend mit dem heutigen Morgen,"

said Alice a little timidly: 48.3
sagte Alice ein wenig zaghaft:

48.4 "but it's no use going back to yesterday, because I was a different person then."

"Aber es hat keinen Sinn, bis gestern zurückzugehen, denn da war ich ein anderer Mensch."

49.1 "Explain all that," said the Mock Turtle.

"Erklären Sie das alles," sagte die falsche Schildkröte.

50.1 "No, no! The adventures first,"

"Nein, nein! Die Abenteuer zuerst,"

50.2 said the Gryphon in an impatient tone:

sagte der Greif in einem ungeduldigen Ton:

50.3 "explanations take such a dreadful time."

"Erklärungen dauern so furchtbar lange."

51.1 So Alice began telling them her adventures from the time when she first saw the White Rabbit.

So begann Alice, ihnen ihre Abenteuer zu erzählen, die sie erlebt hatte, als sie das weiße Kaninchen zum ersten Mal sah.

51.2 She was a little nervous about it just at first, the two creatures got so close to her, one on each side, and opened their eyes and mouths so very wide, but she gained courage as she went on.

Am Anfang war sie ein wenig nervös, weil die beiden Wesen so nahe an sie herankamen, eines auf jeder Seite, und ihre Augen und Münder so weit öffneten, aber sie wurde immer mutiger.

51.3 Her listeners were perfectly quiet till she got to the part about her repeating

Ihre Zuhörer waren ganz still, bis sie zu der Stelle kam, an der sie der Raupe

"You are old, Father William," 51.4

"Du bist alt, Vater William"

to the Caterpillar, and the words all coming different, 51.5
and then the Mock Turtle drew a long breath, and
said:

sagte, und die Worte kamen alle anders, und dann holte die
falsche Schildkröte tief Luft und sagte:

"That's very curious." 51.6

"Das ist sehr merkwürdig."

"It's all about as curious as it can be," 52.1

"Es ist alles so neugierig, wie es nur sein kann,"

said the Gryphon. 52.2

sagte der Greif.

"It all came different!" 53.1

"Es kam alles anders!"

the Mock Turtle repeated thoughtfully. 53.2

wiederholte die falsche Schildkröte nachdenklich.

"I should like to hear her try and repeat something 53.3
now.

"Ich würde gerne hören, wie sie jetzt versucht, etwas zu
wiederholen.

Tell her to begin." 53.4

Sag ihr, sie soll anfangen."

He looked at the Gryphon as if he thought it had some 53.5
kind of authority over Alice.

Er schaute den Greifen an, als ob er glaubte, er hätte eine
Art Autorität über Alice.

54.1 "Stand up and repeat "Tis the voice of the sluggard, "'
Steh auf und wiederhole: "Es ist die Stimme des
Faulenzers,"

54.2 said the Gryphon.
sagte der Greifen.

55.1 "How the creatures order one about,
"Wie die Kreaturen einen herumkommandieren und einen
dazu bringen,

55.2 and make one repeat lessons!" thought Alice;
Lektionen zu wiederholen!" dachte Alice;

55.3 "I might as well be at school at once."
"ich könnte genauso gut sofort in der Schule sein."

55.4 However, she got up, and began to repeat it, but her
head was so full of the Lobster Quadrille, that she
hardly knew what she was saying, and the words
came very queer indeed:-
Aber sie stand auf und begann zu wiederholen, aber ihr
Kopf war so voll von der Hummer-Quadrille, dass sie kaum
wusste, was sie sagte, und die Worte kamen wirklich sehr
seltsam:-

"'Tis the voice of the
Lobster; I heard him
declare,

"'Es ist die Stimme des
Hummers, ich hörte ihn
sagen,

"You have baked me too
brown, I must sugar my
hair."

"Du hast mich zu braun
gebacken, ich muss
meine Haare zuckern."

As a duck with its eyelids, so he with his nose

Wie eine Ente mit ihren Augenlidern, so er mit seiner Nase

Trims his belt and his buttons, and turns out his toes."

Trimmt seinen Gürtel und seine Knöpfe und dreht seine Zehen heraus."

[later editions continued as follows

[Spätere Ausgaben wurden wie folgt fortgesetzt

When the sands are all dry, he is gay as a lark,

Wenn der Sand trocken ist, ist er fröhlich wie eine Lerche,

And will talk in contemptuous tones of the Shark,

Und wird in verächtlichem Ton über den Hai sprechen,

But, when the tide rises and sharks are around,

Aber wenn die Flut steigt und Haie in der Nähe sind,

His voice has a timid and tremulous sound.]

Seine Stimme hat einen schüchternen und zittrigen Klang.]

"That's different from what I used to say when I was a child,"   57.1

"Das ist etwas anderes als das, was ich als Kind immer gesagt habe,"

said the Gryphon.   57.2

sagte der Greif.

242

58.1 "Well, I never heard it before,"
"Nun, ich habe das noch nie gehört,"

58.2 said the Mock Turtle;
sagte die Spottschildkröte,

58.3 "but it sounds uncommon nonsense."
"aber es klingt ungewöhnlich unsinnig."

59.1 Alice said nothing;
Alice sagte nichts;

59.2 she had sat down with her face in her hands,
sie hatte sich mit dem Gesicht in den Händen hingesetzt und fragte sich,

59.3 wondering if anything would ever happen in a natural way again.
ob jemals wieder etwas auf natürliche Weise geschehen würde.

60.1 "I should like to have it explained,"
"Ich würde es gerne erklärt bekommen,"

60.2 said the Mock Turtle.
sagte die falsche Schildkröte.

61.1 "She can't explain it," said the Gryphon hastily.
"Sie kann es nicht erklären," sagte der Greif eilig.

61.2 "Go on with the next verse."
"Mach weiter mit der nächsten Strophe."

"But about his toes?" the Mock Turtle persisted. 62.1

"Aber was ist mit seinen Zehen?" beharrte die
Spottschildkröte.

"How could he turn them out with his nose, you 62.2
know?"

"Wie könnte er sie mit seiner Nase herausdrehen, weißt
du?"

"It's the first position in dancing." 63.1

"Das ist die erste Position beim Tanzen."

Alice said; but was dreadfully puzzled by the whole 63.2
thing, and longed to change the subject.

sagte Alice, die von der ganzen Sache furchtbar verwirrt
war und sich danach sehnte, das Thema zu wechseln.

"Go on with the next verse," 64.1

"Fahren Sie mit der nächsten Strophe fort,"

the Gryphon repeated impatiently: "it begins 64.2

wiederholte der Greif ungeduldig: "Sie beginnt mit

'I passed by his garden. "' 64.3

'Ich ging an seinem Garten vorbei. "'

Alice did not dare to disobey, though she felt sure 65.1
it would all come wrong, and she went on in a
trembling voice:-

Alice wagte es nicht, nicht zu gehorchen, obwohl sie sich
sicher war, dass alles schiefgehen würde, und fuhr mit
zitternder Stimme fort:-

"I passed by his garden, and marked, with one eye,

"Ich ging an seinem Garten vorbei und markierte ihn mit einem Auge,

How the Owl and the Panther were sharing a pie — "

Wie die Eule und der Panther sich einen Kuchen teilten ..."

[later editions continued as follows

[Spätere Ausgaben wurden wie folgt fortgesetzt

The Panther took pie-crust, and gravy, and meat,

Der Panther nahm die Pastetenkruste, die Soße und das Fleisch,

While the Owl had the dish as its share of the treat.

Während die Eule die Schale als ihren Teil der Belohnung bekam.

When the pie was all finished, the Owl, as a boon,

Als die Torte fertig war, kam die Eule, als Segen,

Was kindly permitted to pocket the spoon:

Er durfte freundlicherweise den Löffel einstecken:

While the Panther received knife and fork with a growl,

Während der Panther Messer und Gabel mit einem Knurren entgegennahm,

And concluded the banquet -]

Und beendete das Bankett -]

67.1 "What is the use of repeating all that stuff,"
"Was nützt es, das alles zu wiederholen,"

the Mock Turtle interrupted,   67.2
unterbrach ihn die falsche Schildkröte,

"if you don't explain it as you go on?   67.3
"wenn du es nicht erklärst, während du fortfährst?

It's by far the most confusing thing I ever heard!"   67.4
Das ist bei weitem das Verwirrendste, was ich je gehört
habe!"

"Yes, I think you'd better leave off,"   68.1
"Ja, ich glaube, du gehst jetzt besser,"

said the Gryphon: and Alice was only too   68.2
glad to do so.
sagte der Greif, und Alice tat das nur zu gern.

"Shall we try another figure of the Lobster   69.1
Quadrille?"
"Sollen wir eine andere Figur der Hummer-Quadrille
versuchen?"

the Gryphon went on.   69.2
fuhr der Greif fort.

"Or would you like the Mock Turtle to sing you a   69.3
song?"
"Oder möchtest du, dass die falsche Schildkröte dir ein Lied
vorsingt?"

"Oh, a song, please, if the Mock Turtle would be so   70.1
kind,"
"Oh, ein Lied, bitte, wenn die Spottschildkröte so nett
wäre,"

70.2 Alice replied, so eagerly that the Gryphon said, in a rather offended tone:

antwortete Alice so eifrig, dass der Greif in einem etwas beleidigten Ton sagte:

70.3 "Hm! No accounting for tastes! Sing her

"Hm! Über Geschmack lässt sich nicht streiten! Sing ihr

70.4 'Turtle Soup,' will you, old fellow?"

'Schildkrötensuppe,' ja, alter Freund?"

71.1 The Mock Turtle sighed deeply, and began, in a voice sometimes choked with sobs, to sing this:-

Die Spottschildkröte seufzte tief und begann mit einer Stimme, die manchmal von Schluchzern erstickt wurde, folgendes zu singen:-

"Beautiful Soup, so rich and green,

"Schöne Suppe, so reichhaltig und grün,

Waiting in a hot tureen!

Wartet in einer heißen Terrine!

Who for such dainties would not stoop?

Wer würde sich für solche Leckerbissen nicht bücken?

Soup of the evening, beautiful Soup!

Suppe des Abends, schöne Suppe!

Soup of the evening, beautiful Soup!

Suppe des Abends, schöne Suppe!

Beau — ootiful Soo — oop!

Wunderschöner Soo-oop!

Beau — ootiful Soo — oop!

Wunderschöner Soo-oop!

Soo — oop of the e — e — evening,

Soo-oop des e-e-e-Abends,

Beautiful, beautiful Soup!

Schöne, schöne Suppe!

"Beautiful Soup! Who cares for fish,

"Schöne Suppe! Wer kümmert sich um Fisch,

Game, or any other dish?

Wild, oder ein anderes Gericht?

Who would not give all else for two p

Wer würde nicht alles geben für zwei p

ennyworth only of beautiful Soup?

ennyworth nur der schönen Suppe?

Pennyworth only of beautiful Soup?

Pennyworth nur von schöner Suppe?

Beau — ootiful Soo — oop!

Wunderschöner Soo-oop!

Beau — ootiful Soo — oop!

Wunderschöner Soo-oop!

Soo — oop of the e — e — evening,

Soo-oop des e-e-e-Abends,

Beautiful, beauti — FUL SOUP!"

Schöne, schöne Suppe!"

"Chorus again!"
"Noch einmal den Refrain,"

73.1

248

73.2 cried the Gryphon, and the Mock Turtle had just begun to repeat it, when a cry of

rief der Greif, und die falsche Schildkröte hatte gerade begonnen, ihn zu wiederholen, als in der Ferne der Ruf

73.3 "The trial's beginning!" was heard in the distance.

"Der Prozess beginnt" zu hören war.

74.1 "Come on!"

"Komm!"

74.2 cried the Gryphon, and, taking Alice by the hand, it hurried off, without waiting for the end of the song.

rief der Greif, nahm Alice bei der Hand und eilte davon, ohne das Ende des Liedes abzuwarten.

75.1 "What trial is it?"

"Was für eine Prüfung ist das?"

75.2 Alice panted as she ran;

Alice keuchte, während sie rannte;

75.3 but the Gryphon only answered "Come on!"

aber der Greif antwortete nur: "Komm schon!"

75.4 and ran the faster, while more and more faintly came, carried on the breeze that followed them, the melancholy words:-

und rannte noch schneller, während immer leiser, getragen von der Brise, die sie verfolgte, die melancholischen Worte kamen:-

"Soo — oop of the e — e — evening,

Beautiful, beautiful Soup!"

"Soo — oop of the e — e — evening,

Schöne, schöne Suppe!"

CHAPTER XI. Who Stole the Tarts?

KAPITEL XI. Wer hat die Torten gestohlen?

1.1 The King and Queen of Hearts were seated on their throne when they arrived, with a great crowd assembled about them -

Der Herzkönig und die Herzkönigin saßen auf ihrem Thron, als sie ankamen, und eine große Menschenmenge war um sie herum versammelt -

1.2 all sorts of little birds and beasts, as well as the whole pack of cards: the Knave was standing before them, in chains, with a soldier on each side to guard him;

alle möglichen kleinen Vögel und Tiere sowie das ganze Kartenspiel;

1.3 and near the King was the White Rabbit, with a trumpet in one hand, and a scroll of parchment in the other.

Der Knappe stand in Ketten vor ihnen, mit einem Soldaten auf jeder Seite, der ihn bewachte, und neben dem König stand das weiße Kaninchen mit einer Trompete in der einen und einer Pergamentrolle in der anderen Hand.

In the very middle of the court was a table, with a large dish of tarts upon it: they looked so good, that it made Alice quite hungry to look at them —

1.4

In der Mitte des Hofes stand ein Tisch mit einer großen Schüssel voller Torten, die so lecker aussahen, dass Alice schon beim Anblick hungrig wurde —

"I wish they'd get the trial done," she thought, "and hand round the refreshments!"

1.5

"Ich wünschte, die Verhandlung wäre bald vorbei", dachte sie, "und die Erfrischungen würden verteilt!"

But there seemed to be no chance of this, so she began looking at everything about her, to pass away the time.

1.6

Aber das schien aussichtslos zu sein, also begann sie, sich alles um sich herum anzusehen, um sich die Zeit zu vertreiben.

Alice had never been in a court of justice before, but she had read about them in books, and she was quite pleased to find that she knew the name of nearly everything there.

2.1

Alice war noch nie in einem Gerichtssaal gewesen, aber sie hatte in Büchern darüber gelesen, und sie war sehr erfreut, als sie feststellte, dass sie den Namen von fast allem dort kannte.

"That's the judge," she said to herself,

2.2

"Das ist der Richter," sagte sie zu sich selbst,

"because of his great wig."

2.3

"wegen seiner großen Perücke."

The judge, by the way, was the King;

3.1

Der Richter war übrigens der König;

3.2 and as he wore his crown over the wig, (look at the frontispiece if you want to see how he did it,) he did not look at all comfortable, and it was certainly not becoming.

und da er seine Krone über der Perücke trug (schauen Sie sich das Titelbild an, wenn Sie sehen wollen, wie er das gemacht hat), sah er überhaupt nicht bequem aus, und es stand ihm sicher nicht.

4.1 "And that's the jury-box," thought Alice,

"Und das ist der Geschworenenkasten," dachte Alice,

4.2 "and those twelve creatures," (she was obliged to say

"und diese zwölf Kreaturen" (sie musste

4.3 "creatures,"

"Kreaturen"

4.4 you see, because some of them were animals, and some were birds,)

sagen, denn einige von ihnen waren Tiere und andere Vögel,)

4.5 "I suppose they are the jurors."

"das sind wohl die Geschworenen."

4.6 She said this last word two or three times over to herself, being rather proud of it: for she thought, and rightly too, that very few little girls of her age knew the meaning of it at all.

Dieses letzte Wort sagte sie zwei - oder dreimal zu sich selbst und war ziemlich stolz darauf, denn sie dachte zu Recht, dass nur sehr wenige kleine Mädchen in ihrem Alter die Bedeutung dieses Wortes kannten.

4.7 However, "jury-men" would have done just as well.

Aber "Geschworene" hätte es genauso gut getan.

The twelve jurors were all writing very busily on slates.

5.1

Die zwölf Geschworenen schrieben alle sehr eifrig auf Schiefertafeln.

"What are they doing?" Alice whispered to the Gryphon.

5.2

"Was machen die da?" flüsterte Alice dem Greifen zu.

"They can't have anything to put down yet,

5.3

"Sie können noch nichts aufschreiben,

before the trial's begun."

5.4

bevor die Verhandlung begonnen hat."

"They're putting down their names,"

6.1

"Sie schreiben ihre Namen auf,"

the Gryphon whispered in reply,

6.2

flüsterte der Greif zur Antwort,

"for fear they should forget them before the end of the trial."

6.3

"aus Angst, sie könnten sie vor dem Ende des Prozesses vergessen."

"Stupid things!"

7.1

"Dummes Zeug!"

Alice began in a loud, indignant voice, but she stopped hastily, for the White Rabbit cried out:

7.2

begann Alice mit lauter, empörter Stimme, aber sie hörte schnell auf, denn das Weiße Kaninchen rief:

"Silence in the court!"

7.3

"Ruhe im Hof!"

7.4 and the King put on his spectacles and looked anxiously round, to make out who was talking.

und der König setzte seine Brille auf und schaute sich ängstlich um, um zu sehen, wer da sprach.

8.1 Alice could see, as well as if she were looking over their shoulders, that all the jurors were writing down

Alice konnte so gut sehen, als würde sie ihnen über die Schulter schauen, dass alle Geschworenen

8.2 "stupid things!"

"Dummheiten"

8.3 on their slates, and she could even make out that one of them didn't know how to spell

auf ihre Tafeln schrieben, und sie konnte sogar erkennen, dass einer von ihnen nicht wusste, wie man

8.4 "stupid,"

"dumm"

8.5 and that he had to ask his neighbour to tell him.

schreibt, und dass er seinen Nachbarn bitten musste, es ihm zu sagen.

8.6 "A nice muddle their slates'll be in before the trial's over!"

"Ein schönes Durcheinander auf den Schiefertafeln, bevor der Prozess zu Ende ist,"

8.7 thought Alice.

dachte Alice.

9.1 One of the jurors had a pencil that squeaked.

Einer der Geschworenen hatte einen Bleistift, der quietschte.

This of course, Alice could not stand, and she went round the court and got behind him, and very soon found an opportunity of taking it away.

9.2

Das konnte Alice natürlich nicht dulden, und sie ging um das Gericht herum, stellte sich hinter ihn und fand sehr bald eine Gelegenheit, ihn wegzunehmen.

She did it so quickly that the poor little juror (it was Bill, the Lizard) could not make out at all what had become of it; so, after hunting all about for it, he was obliged to write with one finger for the rest of the day; and this was of very little use, as it left no mark on the slate.

9.3

Sie tat es so schnell, dass der arme kleine Geschworene (es war Bill, die Eidechse) überhaupt nicht erkennen konnte, was aus dem Stift geworden war; und so musste er, nachdem er ihn überall gesucht hatte, den Rest des Tages mit einem Finger schreiben, was ihm aber wenig nützte, da er keine Spuren auf der Schiefertafel hinterließ.

"Herald, read the accusation!" said the King.

10.1

"Herold, lies die Anklage!" sagte der König.

On this the White Rabbit blew three blasts on the trumpet, and then unrolled the parchment scroll, and read as follows:-

11.1

Daraufhin blies das Weiße Kaninchen dreimal in die Trompete, entrollte die Pergamentrolle und las vor:-

"The Queen of Hearts, she made some tarts,

"Die Herzkönigin hat ein paar Törtchen gebacken,

All on a summer day:

Und das alles an einem Sommertag:

The Knave of Hearts, he stole those tarts,

Der Herzbube, er hat die Torten gestohlen,

And took them quite away!"

Und nahm sie ganz weg!"

13.1 "Consider your verdict,"
"Überlegen Sie sich Ihr Urteil,"

13.2 the King said to the jury.
sagte der König zu den Geschworenen.

14.1 "Not yet, not yet!" the Rabbit hastily interrupted.
"Noch nicht, noch nicht!" unterbrach das Kaninchen hastig.

14.2 "There's a great deal to come before that!"
"Davor gibt es noch eine Menge zu tun!"

15.1 "Call the first witness,"
"Ruft den ersten Zeugen,"

15.2 said the King; and the White Rabbit blew three blasts on the trumpet, and called out:
sagte der König, und das weiße Kaninchen blies dreimal in die Trompete und rief:

15.3 "First witness!"
"Erster Zeuge!"

16.1 The first witness was the Hatter.
Der erste Zeuge war der Hutmacher.

He came in with a teacup in one hand and a piece of bread-and-butter in the other.

16.2

Er kam mit einer Teetasse in der einen und einem Stück Butterbrot in der anderen Hand herein.

"I beg pardon, your Majesty," he began,

16.3

"Ich bitte um Verzeihung, Eure Majestät," begann er,

"for bringing these in: but I hadn't quite finished my tea when I was sent for."

16.4

"dass ich das hier mitbringe, aber ich hatte meinen Tee noch nicht ganz ausgetrunken, als man nach mir schickte."

"You ought to have finished," said the King.

17.1

"Du hättest fertig werden müssen," sagte der König.

"When did you begin?"

17.2

"Wann hast du angefangen?"

The Hatter looked at the March Hare, who had followed him into the court, arm-in-arm with the Dormouse.

18.1

Der Hutmacher sah den Märzhasen an, der ihm Arm in Arm mit der Haselmaus in den Hof gefolgt war.

"Fourteenth of March, I think it was," he said.

18.2

"Der vierzehnte März, glaube ich, war es," sagte er.

"Fifteenth," said the March Hare.

19.1

"Fünfzehnter," sagte der Märzhase.

"Sixteenth," added the Dormouse.

20.1

"Sechzehnter," fügte die Haselmaus hinzu.

21.1 "Write that down,"

"Schreiben Sie das auf,"

21.2 the King said to the jury, and the jury eagerly wrote down all three dates on their slates, and then added them up, and reduced the answer to shillings and pence.

sagte der König zu den Geschworenen, und die Geschworenen schrieben eifrig alle drei Daten auf ihre Schiefertafeln, addierten sie und reduzierten die Antwort auf Schillinge und Pence.

22.1 "Take off your hat," the King said to the Hatter.

"Nimm deinen Hut ab," sagte der König zum Hutmacher.

23.1 "It isn't mine," said the Hatter.

"Es ist nicht meins," sagte der Hutmacher.

24.1 "Stolen!"

"Gestohlen!"

24.2 the King exclaimed, turning to the jury, who instantly made a memorandum of the fact.

rief der König aus und wandte sich an die Geschworenen, die sich sofort einen Vermerk über diese Tatsache machten.

25.1 "I keep them to sell,"

"Ich behalte sie, um sie zu verkaufen,"

25.2 the Hatter added as an explanation;

fügte der Hutmacher als Erklärung hinzu,

25.3 "I've none of my own. I'm a hatter."

"ich habe keine eigenen. Ich bin ein Hutmacher."

Here the Queen put on her spectacles, and began staring at the Hatter, who turned pale and fidgeted.

26.1

Hier setzte die Königin ihre Brille auf und starrte den Hutmacher an, der blass wurde und zappelte.

"Give your evidence," said the King;

27.1

"Geben Sie Ihre Aussage," sagte der König,

"and don't be nervous,

27.2

"und seien Sie nicht nervös,

or I'll have you executed on the spot."

27.3

sonst lasse ich Sie auf der Stelle hinrichten."

This did not seem to encourage the witness at all:

28.1

Dies schien den Zeugen keineswegs zu ermutigen:

he kept shifting from one foot to the other, looking uneasily at the Queen, and in his confusion he bit a large piece out of his teacup instead of the bread-and-butter.

28.2

Er wippte ständig von einem Fuß auf den anderen, schaute die Königin unruhig an und biss in seiner Verwirrung ein großes Stück aus seiner Teetasse, anstatt das Butterbrot zu essen.

Just at this moment Alice felt a very curious sensation, which puzzled her a good deal until she made out what it was:

29.1

Gerade in diesem Moment spürte Alice ein sehr merkwürdiges Gefühl, das sie sehr verwirrte, bis sie herausfand, was es war:

29.2 she was beginning to grow larger again, and she thought at first she would get up and leave the court;
Sie begann wieder größer zu werden, und sie dachte zuerst, sie würde aufstehen und den Hof verlassen;

29.3 but on second thoughts she decided to remain where she was as long as there was room for her.
aber nach reiflicher Überlegung beschloss sie, dort zu bleiben, wo sie war, solange es Platz für sie gab.

30.1 "I wish you wouldn't squeeze so."
"Ich wünschte, du würdest dich nicht so quetschen."

30.2 said the Dormouse, who was sitting next to her.
sagte die Haselmaus, die neben ihr saß.

30.3 "I can hardly breathe."
"Ich kann kaum noch atmen."

31.1 "I can't help it," said Alice very meekly:
"Ich kann nichts dafür," sagte Alice ganz kleinlaut:

31.2 "I'm growing."
"Ich wachse."

32.1 "You've no right to grow here," said the Dormouse.
"Du hast kein Recht, hier zu wachsen," sagte die Haselmaus.

33.1 "Don't talk nonsense," said Alice more boldly:
"Rede keinen Unsinn," sagte Alice mutiger:

33.2 "you know you're growing too."
"du weißt, dass du auch wächst."

"Yes, but I grow at a reasonable pace," 34.1
"Ja, aber ich wachse in einem vernünftigen Tempo,"

said the Dormouse: 34.2
sagte die Haselmaus:

"not in that ridiculous fashion." 34.3
"nicht auf diese lächerliche Art und Weise."

And he got up very sulkily and crossed over to the 34.4
other side of the court.
Und er stand sehr mürrisch auf und ging auf die andere
Seite des Platzes.

All this time the Queen had never left off staring at 35.1
the Hatter, and, just as the Dormouse crossed the
court, she said to one of the officers of the court,
Während der ganzen Zeit hatte die Königin nicht aufgehört,
den Hutmacher anzustarren, und gerade als die Haselmaus
den Hof überquerte, sagte sie zu einem der Hofbeamten:

"Bring me the list of the singers in the last concert!" 35.2
"Bringt mir die Liste der Sänger des letzten Konzerts!"

on which the wretched Hatter trembled so, 35.3
worauf der unglückliche Hutmacher so zitterte,

that he shook both his shoes off. 35.4
dass er beide Schuhe abschüttelte.

"Give your evidence," the King repeated angrily, 36.1
"Geben Sie Ihre Beweise ab," wiederholte der König
wütend,

"or I'll have you executed, 36.2
"oder ich lasse Sie hinrichten,

36.3 **whether you're nervous or not."**
ob Sie nun nervös sind oder nicht."

37.1 **"I'm a poor man, your Majesty,"**
"Ich bin ein armer Mann, Eure Majestät,"

37.2 **the Hatter began, in a trembling voice,**
begann der Hutmacher mit zitternder Stimme,

37.3 **" — and I hadn't begun my tea — not above a week or so — and what with the bread-and-butter getting so thin — and the twinkling of the tea — "**
"und ich habe seit einer Woche nicht mehr mit dem Tee angefangen, und weil das Brot und die Butter so dünn geworden sind und der Tee so schlecht geworden ist ..."

38.1 **"The twinkling of the what?" said the King.**
"Das Zwinkern von was?" sagte der König.

39.1 **"It began with the tea," the Hatter replied.**
"Es begann mit dem Tee," antwortete der Hutmacher.

40.1 **"Of course twinkling begins with a T!"**
"Natürlich beginnt das Zwinkern mit einem T!"

40.2 **said the King sharply. "Do you take me for a dunce?**
sagte der König scharf. "Hältst du mich für einen Dummkopf?

40.3 **Go on!"**
Fahren Sie fort!"

41.1 **"I'm a poor man," the Hatter went on,**
"Ich bin ein armer Mann," fuhr der Hutmacher fort,

"and most things twinkled after that — only the March Hare said — "

41.2

"und die meisten Dinge haben danach geglitzert - nur der Märzhase sagte ..."

"I didn't!" the March Hare interrupted in a great hurry.

42.1

"Das habe ich nicht!" unterbrach der Märzhase in großer Eile.

"You did!" said the Hatter.

43.1

"Das hast du!" sagte der Hutmacher.

"I deny it!" said the March Hare.

44.1

"Ich leugne es!" sagte der Märzhase.

"He denies it," said the King: "leave out that part."

45.1

"Er leugnet es," sagte der König, "lassen Sie diesen Teil weg."

"Well, at any rate, the Dormouse said — "

46.1

"Jedenfalls hat die Haselmaus gesagt — ,"

the Hatter went on, looking anxiously round to see if he would deny it too: but the Dormouse denied nothing, being fast asleep.

46.2

fuhr der Hutmacher fort und schaute sich ängstlich um, um zu sehen, ob er es auch leugnen würde; aber die Haselmaus leugnete nichts, da sie fest schlief.

"After that," continued the Hatter,

47.1

"Danach," fuhr der Hutmacher fort,

47.2   "I cut some more bread-and- butter — "
"schnitt ich noch etwas Butterbrot ..."

48.1   "But what did the Dormouse say?"
"Aber was hat die Haselmaus gesagt?"

48.2   one of the jury asked.
fragte einer der Geschworenen.

49.1   "That I can't remember," said the Hatter.
"Daran kann ich mich nicht erinnern," sagte der
Hutmacher.

50.1   "You must remember," remarked the King,
"Sie müssen daran denken," bemerkte der König,

50.2   "or I'll have you executed."
"oder ich lasse Sie hinrichten."

51.1   The miserable Hatter dropped his teacup and bread-
and-butter, and went down on one knee.
Der unglückliche Hutmacher ließ seine Teetasse und sein
Butterbrot fallen und ging auf ein Knie nieder.

51.2   "I'm a poor man, your Majesty," he began.
"Ich bin ein armer Mann, Eure Majestät," begann er.

52.1   "You're a very poor speaker," said the King.
"Sie sind ein sehr schlechter Redner," sagte der König.

53.1   Here one of the guinea-pigs cheered, and was
immediately suppressed by the officers of the court.
Hier jubelte eines der Meerschweinchen und wurde sofort
von den Hofbeamten unterdrückt.

(As that is rather a hard word, I will just explain to you how it was done.   53.2

(Da das ein ziemlich hartes Wort ist, werde ich euch einfach erklären, wie es gemacht wurde.

They had a large canvas bag, which tied up at the mouth with strings: into this they slipped the guinea-pig, head first, and then sat upon it.)   53.3

Sie hatten einen großen Leinensack, der an der Öffnung mit Schnüren zugebunden war; in diesen Sack steckten sie das Meerschweinchen mit dem Kopf voran und setzten sich dann darauf.)

"I'm glad I've seen that done," thought Alice.   54.1

"Ich bin froh, dass ich das gesehen habe," dachte Alice.

"I've so often read in the newspapers, at the end of trials,   54.2

"Ich habe so oft in den Zeitungen am Ende von Prozessen gelesen:

"There was some attempts at applause, which was immediately suppressed by the officers of the court,"   54.3

"Es gab einige Versuche, Beifall zu klatschen, die sofort von den Gerichtsbeamten unterdrückt wurden,"

and I never understood what it meant till now."   54.4

und ich habe bis jetzt nie verstanden, was das bedeutet."

"If that's all you know about it, you may stand down,"   55.1

"Wenn das alles ist, was Sie darüber wissen, können Sie sich zurückziehen,"

continued the King.   55.2

fuhr der König fort.

56.1 "I can't go no lower," said the Hatter:
"Tiefer kann ich nicht mehr gehen," sagte der Hutmacher:

56.2 "I'm on the floor, as it is."
"Ich bin sowieso schon auf dem Boden."

57.1 "Then you may sit down," the King replied.
"Dann können Sie sich setzen," antwortete der König.

58.1 Here the other guinea-pig cheered, and was suppressed.
Hier jubelte das andere Meerschweinchen, und wurde unterdrückt.

59.1 "Come, that finished the guinea-pigs!" thought Alice.
"Komm, das war's mit den Meerschweinchen!" dachte Alice.

59.2 "Now we shall get on better."
"Jetzt werden wir besser vorankommen."

60.1 "I'd rather finish my tea,"
"Ich trinke lieber meinen Tee aus,"

60.2 said the Hatter, with an anxious look at the Queen, who was reading the list of singers.
sagte der Hutmacher mit einem besorgten Blick auf die Königin, die gerade die Liste der Sänger las.

61.1 "You may go,"
"Ihr könnt gehen,"

said the King, and the Hatter hurriedly left the court, without even waiting to put his shoes on.   61.2

sagte der König, und der Hutmacher verließ eilig den Hof, ohne darauf zu warten, seine Schuhe anzuziehen.

" — and just take his head off outside, "   62.1

"Und köpft ihn einfach draußen, "

the Queen added to one of the officers: but the Hatter was out of sight before the officer could get to the door.   62.2

fügte die Königin zu einem der Offiziere hinzu, aber der Hutmacher war außer Sichtweite, bevor der Offizier zur Tür gelangen konnte.

"Call the next witness!" said the King.   63.1

"Rufen Sie den nächsten Zeugen auf!" sagte der König.

The next witness was the Duchess's cook.   64.1

Die nächste Zeugin war die Köchin der Herzogin.

She carried the pepper-box in her hand, and Alice guessed who it was, even before she got into the court, by the way the people near the door began sneezing all at once.   64.2

Sie trug die Pfefferbüchse in der Hand, und Alice ahnte, wer es war, noch bevor sie den Saal betrat, weil die Leute in der Nähe der Tür auf einmal zu niesen begannen.

"Give your evidence, " said the King.   65.1

"Geben Sie Ihr Zeugnis, " sagte der König.

"Shan't, " said the cook.   66.1

"Nein, " sagte der Koch.

67.1 **The King looked anxiously at the White Rabbit, who said in a low voice:**

Der König blickte besorgt auf das Weiße Kaninchen, das mit leiser Stimme sagte:

67.2 **"Your Majesty must cross-examine this witness."**

"Eure Majestät müssen diesen Zeugen ins Kreuzverhör nehmen."

68.1 **"Well, if I must, I must,"**

"Nun, wenn es sein muss, muss es sein,"

68.2 **the King said, with a melancholy air, and, after folding his arms and frowning at the cook till his eyes were nearly out of sight, he said in a deep voice:**

sagte der König mit melancholischer Miene, und nachdem er die Arme verschränkt und den Koch stirnrunzelnd angestarrt hatte, bis seine Augen fast nicht mehr zu sehen waren, sagte er mit tiefer Stimme:

68.3 **"What are tarts made of?"**

"Woraus sind Torten gemacht?"

69.1 **"Pepper, mostly," said the cook.**

"Hauptsächlich Pfeffer," sagte der Koch.

70.1 **"Treacle," said a sleepy voice behind her.**

"Treacle," sagte eine schläfrige Stimme hinter ihr.

71.1 **"Collar that Dormouse," the Queen shrieked out.**

"Legt der Haselmaus das Halsband an," schrie die Königin.

"Behead that Dormouse! Turn that Dormouse out of court!

71.2

"Enthauptet die Haselmaus! Schmeißt die Haselmaus aus dem Hof!

Suppress him! Pinch him! Off with his whiskers!"

71.3

Unterdrückt ihn! Kneift ihn! Weg mit den Schnurrhaaren!"

For some minutes the whole court was in confusion, getting the Dormouse turned out, and, by the time they had settled down again, the cook had disappeared.

72.1

Einige Minuten lang war der ganze Hof in Aufruhr, um die Haselmaus herauszubekommen, und als sie sich wieder beruhigt hatten, war der Koch verschwunden.

"Never mind!"

73.1

"Das macht nichts,"

said the King, with an air of great relief.

73.2

sagte der König und wirkte sehr erleichtert.

"Call the next witness."

73.3

"Rufen Sie den nächsten Zeugen auf."

And he added in an undertone to the Queen,

73.4

Und er fügte in einem Unterton zur Königin hinzu:

"Really, my dear, you must cross-examine the next witness.

73.5

"Wirklich, meine Liebe, Sie müssen den nächsten Zeugen ins Kreuzverhör nehmen.

It quite makes my forehead ache!"

73.6

Mir tut schon die Stirn weh!"

74.1 Alice watched the White Rabbit as he fumbled over the list, feeling very curious to see what the next witness would be like,

Alice beobachtete das Weiße Kaninchen, während es die Liste durchblätterte, und war sehr neugierig, wie der nächste Zeuge aussehen würde,

74.2 " — for they haven't got much evidence yet,"

"denn sie haben noch nicht viele Beweise,"

74.3 she said to herself.

sagte sie zu sich selbst.

74.4 Imagine her surprise, when the White Rabbit read out, at the top of his shrill little voice, the name:

Stellen Sie sich ihre Überraschung vor, als das Weiße Kaninchen mit schriller kleiner Stimme den Namen vorlas:

74.5 "Alice!"

"Alice!"

CHAPTER XII. Alice's Evidence

KAPITEL XII. Alices Beweise

1.1 "Here!"
"Hier!"

1.2 cried Alice, quite forgetting in the flurry of the moment how large she had grown in the last few minutes, and she jumped up in such a hurry that she tipped over the jury-box with the edge of her skirt, upsetting all the jurymen on to the heads of the crowd below, and there they lay sprawling about, reminding her very much of a globe of goldfish she had accidentally upset the week before.
rief Alice, die in der Aufregung des Augenblicks ganz vergaß, wie groß sie in den letzten Minuten geworden war, und sie sprang so eilig auf, dass sie mit dem Rand ihres Rocks den Geschworenenkasten umwarf, wodurch alle Geschworenen auf die Köpfe der Menge unten stürzten, und dort lagen sie herum und erinnerten sie sehr an eine Kugel Goldfische, die sie in der Woche zuvor versehentlich umgeworfen hatte.

2.1 "Oh, I beg your pardon!"
"Oh, ich bitte um Verzeihung!"

she exclaimed in a tone of great dismay, and began picking them up again as quickly as she could, for the accident of the goldfish kept running in her head, and she had a vague sort of idea that they must be collected at once and put back into the jury-box, or they would die.

2.2

rief sie mit großer Bestürzung aus und begann, sie so schnell wie möglich wieder einzusammeln, denn der Unfall der Goldfische ging ihr nicht aus dem Kopf, und sie hatte eine vage Vorstellung davon, dass sie sofort eingesammelt und zurück in die Jury-Box gelegt werden müssten, sonst würden sie sterben.

"The trial cannot proceed,"

3.1

"Die Verhandlung kann nicht fortgesetzt werden,"

said the King in a very grave voice,

3.2

sagte der König mit sehr ernster Stimme,

"until all the jurymen are back in their proper places - all,"

3.3

"bis alle Geschworenen wieder an ihrem Platz sind - alle,"

he repeated with great emphasis, looking hard at Alice as he said so.

3.4

wiederholte er mit großem Nachdruck und sah Alice dabei scharf an.

Alice looked at the jury-box, and saw that, in her haste, she had put the Lizard in head downwards, and the poor little thing was waving its tail about in a melancholy way, being quite unable to move.

4.1

Alice schaute in den Geschworenenkasten und sah, dass sie in ihrer Eile die Eidechse mit dem Kopf nach unten hineingesteckt hatte, und das arme kleine Ding wedelte melancholisch mit dem Schwanz herum, weil es sich nicht bewegen konnte.

4.2 She soon got it out again, and put it right;
Sie holte sie bald wieder heraus und setzte sie richtig ein;

4.3 "not that it signifies much,"
"nicht, dass das viel zu bedeuten hätte,"

4.4 she said to herself;
sagte sie zu sich selbst;

4.5 "I should think it would be quite as much use in the trial one way up as the other."
"ich denke, sie wäre in der Verhandlung mit dem Kopf nach oben genauso nützlich wie mit dem Kopf nach unten."

5.1 As soon as the jury had a little recovered from the shock of being upset, and their slates and pencils had been found and handed back to them, they set to work very diligently to write out a history of the accident, all except the Lizard, who seemed too much overcome to do anything but sit with its mouth open, gazing up into the roof of the court.
Sobald sich die Geschworenen ein wenig von dem Schock erholt hatten und ihre Schiefertafeln und Stifte gefunden und zurückgegeben worden waren, machten sie sich eifrig an die Arbeit, um eine Geschichte des Unfalls zu schreiben, alle außer der Eidechse, die zu überwältigt schien, um irgendetwas anderes zu tun, als mit offenem Mund dazusitzen und zum Dach des Gerichts hinaufzustarren.

6.1 "What do you know about this business?" the King said to Alice.
"Was wissen Sie über dieses Geschäft?" fragte der König Alice.

7.1 "Nothing," said Alice.
"Nichts," sagte Alice.

"Nothing whatever?" persisted the King.   8.1
"Gar nichts?" fragte der König weiter.

"Nothing whatever," said Alice.   9.1
"Gar nichts," sagte Alice.

"That's very important,"   10.1
"Das ist sehr wichtig,"

the King said, turning to the jury.   10.2
sagte der König und wandte sich an die Geschworenen.

They were just beginning to write this down on their   10.3
slates, when the White Rabbit interrupted:
Sie begannen gerade, dies auf ihren Tafeln zu notieren, als
das weiße Kaninchen sie unterbrach:

"Unimportant, your Majesty means, of course,"   10.4
"Unwichtig, meint Eure Majestät natürlich,"

he said in a very respectful tone, but frowning and   10.5
making faces at him as he spoke.
sagte er in einem sehr respektvollen Ton, aber er runzelte
die Stirn und schnitt ihm Grimassen, während er sprach.

"Unimportant, of course, I meant,"   11.1
"Unwichtig, natürlich, meinte ich,"

the King hastily said, and went on to himself in an   11.2
undertone,
sagte der König hastig und fuhr mit einem Unterton zu sich
selbst fort,

12.1 "important — unimportant — unimportant —
important — "
"wichtig-unwichtig-unwichtig-unwichtig - wichtig-,"

12.2 **as if he were trying which word sounded best.**
als ob er ausprobieren würde, welches Wort am besten
klingt.

13.1 **Some of the jury wrote it down "important,"**
Einige der Geschworenen schrieben es als "wichtig,"

13.2 **and some "unimportant."**
andere als "unwichtig" auf."

13.3 **Alice could see this, as she was near enough to look
over their slates;**
Alice konnte dies sehen, da sie nahe genug war, um auf die
Schiefertafeln zu schauen;

13.4 **"but it doesn't matter a bit," she thought to herself.**
"aber das ist völlig egal," dachte sie bei sich.

14.1 **At this moment the King, who had been for some
time busily writing in his note-book, cackled out**
In diesem Moment rief der König, der seit einiger Zeit eifrig
in sein Notizbuch schrieb,

14.2 **"Silence!" and read out from his book, "Rule Forty-
two.**
"Ruhe!" und las aus seinem Buch vor: "Regel
zweiundvierzig.

14.3 **All persons more than a mile high to leave the court."**
Alle Personen, die mehr als eine Meile hoch sind, müssen
den Hof verlassen."

Everybody looked at Alice.   15.1
Alle sahen Alice an.

"I'm not a mile high," said Alice.   16.1
"Ich bin keine Meile hoch," sagte Alice.

"You are," said the King.   17.1
"Das bist du," sagte der König.

"Nearly two miles high," added the Queen.   18.1
"Fast zwei Meilen hoch," fügte die Königin hinzu.

"Well, I shan't go, at any rate," said Alice: 19.1
"Nun, ich werde jedenfalls nicht gehen," sagte Alice:

"besides,   19.2
"außerdem ist das keine normale Regel,

that's not a regular rule: you invented it just now."   19.3
die hast du doch gerade erst erfunden."

"It's the oldest rule in the book," said the King.   20.1
"Das ist die älteste Regel im Buch," sagte der König.

"Then it ought to be Number One," said Alice.   21.1
"Dann sollte es Nummer Eins sein," sagte Alice.

The King turned pale, and shut his note-book hastily.   22.1
Der König wurde blass und schloss hastig sein Notizbuch.

"Consider your verdict,"   22.2
"Überlegen Sie sich Ihr Urteil,"

22.3 he said to the jury, in a low, trembling voice.
sagte er mit leiser, zitternder Stimme zu den
Geschworenen.

23.1 "There's more evidence to come yet, please your
Majesty,"
"Es gibt noch mehr Beweise, bitte, Eure Majestät,"

23.2 said the White Rabbit, jumping up in a great hurry;
sagte das weiße Kaninchen und sprang eilig auf;

23.3 "this paper has just been picked up."
"diese Zeitung wurde gerade abgeholt."

24.1 "What's in it?" said the Queen.
"Was ist da drin?" fragte die Königin.

25.1 "I haven't opened it yet," said the White Rabbit,
"Ich habe ihn noch nicht geöffnet," sagte das weiße
Kaninchen,

25.2 "but it seems to be a letter,
"aber es scheint ein Brief zu sein,

25.3 written by the prisoner to — to somebody."
den der Gefangene an jemanden geschrieben hat."

26.1 "It must have been that," said the King,
"Das muss es gewesen sein," sagte der König,

26.2 "unless it was written to nobody, which isn't usual,
you know."
"es sei denn, es wurde an niemanden geschrieben, was
nicht üblich ist, wie Sie wissen."

"Who is it directed to?" said one of the jurymen.   27.1

"An wen ist sie gerichtet?" fragte einer der Geschworenen.

"It isn't directed at all,"   28.1

"Es ist überhaupt nicht an mich gerichtet,"

said the White Rabbit;   28.2

sagte das weiße Kaninchen,

"in fact, there's nothing written on the outside."   28.3

"auf der Außenseite steht gar nichts geschrieben."

He unfolded the paper as he spoke, and added "It isn't   28.4
a letter, after all:

Während er sprach, faltete er das Papier auseinander und
fügte hinzu:

it's a set of verses."   28.5

"Es ist ja kein Brief, sondern eine Reihe von Versen."

"Are they in the prisoner's handwriting?"   29.1

"Sind sie in der Handschrift des Gefangenen?"

asked another of the jurymen.   29.2

fragte ein anderer der Geschworenen.

"No, they're not," said the White Rabbit,   30.1

"Nein, das sind sie nicht," sagte das weiße Kaninchen,

"and that's the queerest thing about it."   30.2

"und das ist das Seltsamste daran."

(The jury all looked puzzled.)   30.3

(Die Geschworenen schauten alle verwirrt.)

31.1 "He must have imitated somebody else's hand,"
"Er muss die Hand eines anderen nachgeahmt haben,"

31.2 said the King. (The jury all brightened up again.)
sagte der König. (Die Geschworenen erheiterten sich wieder.)

32.1 "Please your Majesty," said the Knave,
"Bitte, Eure Majestät," sagte der Knappe,

32.2 "I didn't write it, and they can't prove I did:
"ich habe es nicht geschrieben, und sie können nicht beweisen, dass ich es getan habe:

32.3 there's no name signed at the end."
Es steht kein Name am Ende."

33.1 "If you didn't sign it," said the King,
"Wenn Sie nicht unterschrieben haben," sagte der König,

33.2 "that only makes the matter worse.
"macht das die Sache nur noch schlimmer.

33.3 You must have meant some mischief,
Ihr müsst es böse gemeint haben,

33.4 or else you'd have signed your name like an honest man."
sonst hättet Ihr wie ein ehrlicher Mann unterschrieben."

34.1 There was a general clapping of hands at this: it was the first really clever thing the King had said that day.
Das war das erste wirklich kluge Wort, das der König an diesem Tag gesagt hatte, und es wurde allgemein beklatscht.

"That proves his guilt," said the Queen.   35.1
"Das beweist seine Schuld," sagte die Königin.

"It proves nothing of the sort!" said Alice.   36.1
"Das beweist gar nichts!" sagte Alice.

"Why, you don't even know what they're about!"   36.2
"Du weißt ja nicht einmal, worum es sich handelt!"

"Read them," said the King.   37.1
"Lies sie," sagte der König.

The White Rabbit put on his spectacles.   38.1
Das weiße Kaninchen setzte seine Brille auf.

"Where shall I begin, please your Majesty?" he asked.   38.2
"Wo soll ich anfangen, bitte, Majestät?" fragte er.

"Begin at the beginning," the King said gravely,   39.1
"Fangen Sie am Anfang an," sagte der König ernst,

"and go on till you come to the end: then stop."   39.2
"und fahren Sie fort, bis Sie zum Ende kommen; dann hören Sie auf."

These were the verses the White Rabbit read: — .   40.1
Dies waren die Verse, die das weiße Kaninchen las.

"They told me you had been to her,	"Man hat mir gesagt, dass du bei ihr gewesen bist,
And mentioned me to him:	Und hat mich ihm gegenüber erwähnt:

282

She gave me a good character,	Sie gab mir einen guten Charakter,
But said I could not swim.	Aber er sagte, ich könne nicht schwimmen.
He sent them word I had not gone.	Er ließ sie wissen, dass ich nicht gegangen war.
(We know it to be true):	(Wir wissen, dass es wahr ist):
If she should push the matter on,	Wenn sie die Angelegenheit weiter vorantreiben sollte,
What would become of you?	Was würde aus Ihnen werden?
I gave her one, they gave him two,	Ich habe ihr eine gegeben, sie haben ihm zwei gegeben,
You gave us three or more;	Sie haben uns drei oder mehr gegeben;
They all returned from him to you,	Sie sind alle von ihm zu dir zurückgekehrt,
Though they were mine before.	Auch wenn sie vorher mir gehörten.
If I or she should chance to be	Sollte ich oder sie zufällig
Involved in this affair,	In diese Affäre verwickelt,

He trusts to you to set them free,

Er vertraut darauf, dass Sie sie befreien können,

Exactly as we were.

Genau so, wie wir waren.

My notion was that you had been

Ich hatte den Eindruck, dass Sie

(Before she had this fit)

(Bevor sie diesen Anfall hatte)

An obstacle that came between

Ein Hindernis, das sich zwischen

Him, and ourselves, and it.

Ihn und uns und es.

Don't let him know she liked them best,

Lassen Sie ihn nicht wissen, dass sie sie am liebsten mag,

For this must ever be

Denn das muss immer sein

A secret, kept from all the rest,

Ein Geheimnis, das vor allen anderen geheim gehalten wird,

Between yourself and me."

Das bleibt unter uns."

"That's the most important piece of evidence we've heard yet," 42.1

"Das ist das wichtigste Beweisstück, das wir bisher gehört haben,"

said the King, rubbing his hands; 42.2

sagte der König und rieb sich die Hände;

284

42.3 "so now let the jury — "
"die Geschworenen sollen also — "

43.1 "If any one of them can explain it,"
"Wenn einer von ihnen es erklären kann,"

43.2 said Alice, (she had grown so large in the last few minutes that she wasn't a bit afraid of interrupting him,)
sagte Alice (sie war in den letzten Minuten so groß geworden, dass sie keine Angst hatte, ihn zu unterbrechen,)

43.3 "I'll give him sixpence.
"dann gebe ich ihm einen Sixpence.

43.4 I don't believe there's an atom of meaning in it."
Ich glaube nicht, dass es auch nur ein Atom an Bedeutung hat."

44.1 The jury all wrote down on their slates,
Die Geschworenen schrieben alle auf ihre Tafeln:

44.2 "She doesn't believe there's an atom of meaning in it,"
"Sie glaubt nicht, dass es ein Atom an Bedeutung hat,"

44.3 but none of them attempted to explain the paper.
aber keiner von ihnen versuchte, das Papier zu erklären.

45.1 "If there's no meaning in it," said the King,
"Wenn es keinen Sinn hat," sagte der König,

45.2 "that saves a world of trouble, you know, as we needn't try to find any.
"erspart uns das eine Menge Ärger, denn wir müssen nicht versuchen, einen zu finden.

And yet I don't know," 45.3
Und doch weiß ich nicht,"

he went on, spreading out the verses on his knee, and 45.4
looking at them with one eye;
fuhr er fort, breitete die Verse auf seinem Knie aus und
betrachtete sie mit einem Auge,

"I seem to see some meaning in them, after all. 45.5
"ich scheine doch einen Sinn darin zu sehen.

" — said I could not swim — " you can't swim, can 45.6
you?"
"Du kannst nicht schwimmen, nicht wahr?"

he added, turning to the Knave. 45.7
fügte er hinzu und wandte sich an den Knappen.

The Knave shook his head sadly. "Do I look like it?" 46.1
Der Knappe schüttelte traurig den Kopf. "Sehe ich so aus?"

he said. (Which he certainly did not, 46.2
fragte er. (Was er sicherlich nicht tat,

being made entirely of cardboard.) 46.3
da er ganz aus Pappe war.)

"All right, so far," said the King, 47.1
"So weit, so gut," sagte der König und fuhr fort,

and he went on muttering over the verses to himself: 47.2
die Verse vor sich hin zu murmeln:

47.3 "'We know it to be true — ' that's the jury, of
course — 'I gave her one, they gave him two — '
why, that must be what he did with the tarts, you
know — "

"'Wir wissen, dass es wahr ist,' das sind natürlich die
Geschworenen, 'ich habe ihr eine gegeben, sie haben ihm
zwei gegeben,' das muss es sein, was er mit den Torten
gemacht hat, weißt du?"

48.1 "But, it goes on 'they all returned from him to you,"'
said Alice.

"Aber es geht weiter, sie sind alle von ihm zu dir
zurückgekehrt," sagte Alice.

49.1 "Why, there they are!"

"Da sind sie ja!"

49.2 said the King triumphantly, pointing to the tarts on
the table.

sagte der König triumphierend und zeigte auf die Torten
auf dem Tisch.

49.3 "Nothing can be clearer than that.

"Nichts kann deutlicher sein als das.

49.4 Then again — 'before she had this fit — ' you never
had fits, my dear, I think?"

Andererseits - 'bevor sie diesen Anfall hatte-' du hattest nie
Anfälle, meine Liebe, glaube ich?"

49.5 he said to the Queen.

sagte er zur Königin.

50.1 "Never!"

"Niemals!"

said the Queen furiously, 50.2

sagte die Königin wütend und warf ein Tintenfass nach der Echse,

throwing an inkstand at the Lizard as she spoke. 50.3

während sie sprach.

(The unfortunate little Bill had left off writing on his slate with one finger, as he found it made no mark; 50.4

(Der unglückliche kleine Bill hatte aufgehört, mit einem Finger auf seine Schiefertafel zu schreiben, weil er fand, dass sie keine Spuren hinterließ;

but he now hastily began again, using the ink, that was trickling down his face, as long as it lasted.) 50.5

aber jetzt begann er eilig wieder, indem er die Tinte benutzte, die ihm über das Gesicht tropfte, solange sie reichte.)

"Then the words don't fit you," 51.1

"Dann passen die Worte nicht zu Ihnen,"

said the King, looking round the court with a smile. 51.2

sagte der König und blickte sich lächelnd im Saal um.

There was a dead silence. 51.3

Es herrschte eine Totenstille.

"It's a pun." 52.1

"Das ist ein Wortspiel," fügte der König beleidigt hinzu, woraufhin alle lachten."

52.2 the King added in an offended tone, and everybody laughed, "Let the jury consider their verdict," the King said, for about the twentieth time that day.

"Die Geschworenen sollen sich ihr Urteil überlegen," sagte der König zum ungefähr zwanzigsten Mal an diesem Tag.

53.1 "No, no!" said the Queen.

"Nein, nein!" sagte die Königin.

53.2 "Sentence first — verdict afterwards."

"Erst die Strafe, dann das Urteil."

54.1 "Stuff and nonsense!" said Alice loudly.

"Quatsch und Unsinn!" sagte Alice laut.

54.2 "The idea of having the sentence first!"

"Die Idee, den Satz zuerst zu haben!"

55.1 "Hold your tongue!" said the Queen, turning purple.

"Hüte deine Zunge!" sagte die Königin und wurde rot.

56.1 "I won't!" said Alice.

"Das werde ich nicht!" sagte Alice.

57.1 "Off with her head!" the Queen shouted at the top of her voice.

"Ab mit ihrem Kopf!" schrie die Königin mit lauter Stimme.

57.2 Nobody moved.

Niemand rührte sich.

58.1 "Who cares for you?"

"Wer kümmert sich um dich?"

said Alice, (she had grown to her full size by this time.) 58.2

sagte Alice (sie war inzwischen zu ihrer vollen Größe herangewachsen.)

"You're nothing but a pack of cards!" 58.3

"Du bist nichts als ein Kartenspiel!"

At this the whole pack rose up into the air, and came flying down upon her: she gave a little scream, half of fright and half of anger, and tried to beat them off, and found herself lying on the bank, with her head in the lap of her sister, who was gently brushing away some dead leaves that had fluttered down from the trees upon her face. 59.1

Sie stieß einen kleinen Schrei aus, halb vor Schreck, halb vor Wut, und versuchte, sie wegzuschlagen, und fand sich am Ufer liegend wieder, mit dem Kopf im Schoß ihrer Schwester, die ihr sanft ein paar tote Blätter abbürstete, die von den Bäumen auf ihr Gesicht geflattert waren.

"Wake up, Alice dear!" said her sister; 60.1

"Wach auf, liebe Alice," sagte ihre Schwester,

"Why, what a long sleep you've had!" 60.2

"du hast aber lange geschlafen!"

"Oh, I've had such a curious dream!" 61.1

"Oh, ich habe so seltsam geträumt!"

said Alice, and she told her sister, as well as she could remember them, all these strange Adventures of hers that you have just been reading about; 61.2

sagte Alice, und sie erzählte ihrer Schwester, so gut sie sich erinnern konnte, all diese seltsamen Abenteuer, von denen du gerade gelesen hast;

61.3 and when she had finished, her sister kissed her, and
said, "It was a curious dream, dear, certainly:
und als sie geendet hatte, küsste ihre Schwester sie und
sagte:

61.4 but now run in to your tea;
"Es war ein seltsamer Traum, meine Liebe, gewiss;

61.5 it's getting late."
aber jetzt geh zu deinem Tee, es ist schon spät."

61.6 So Alice got up and ran off, thinking while she ran, as
well she might, what a wonderful dream it had been.
Alice stand auf und lief davon, wobei sie sich dachte, was
für ein wunderbarer Traum das gewesen war.

63.1 But her sister sat still just as she left her, leaning
her head on her hand, watching the setting sun,
and thinking of little Alice and all her wonderful
Adventures, till she too began dreaming after a
fashion, and this was her dream: —
Aber ihre Schwester saß immer noch so da, wie sie sie
verlassen hatte, stützte den Kopf auf ihre Hand, betrachtete
die untergehende Sonne und dachte an die kleine Alice und
all ihre wunderbaren Abenteuer, bis auch sie zu träumen
begann, und dies war ihr Traum: —

64.1 First, she dreamed of little Alice herself, and once
again the tiny hands were clasped upon her knee, and
the bright eager eyes were looking up into hers -
Zuerst träumte sie von der kleinen Alice selbst, und wieder
waren die winzigen Hände auf ihr Knie gelegt, und die
hellen, eifrigen Augen blickten zu den ihren auf -

she could hear the very tones of her voice, and see   64.2
that queer little toss of her head to keep back the
wandering hair that would always get into her eyes -

sie konnte den Klang ihrer Stimme hören und sah, wie sie
ihren Kopf seltsam hin und her wog, um die wandernden
Haare zurückzuhalten, die ihr immer in die Augen fielen -

and still as she listened, or seemed to listen, the   64.3
whole place around her became alive with the strange
creatures of her little sister's dream.

und während sie noch lauschte oder zu lauschen schien,
wurde der ganze Ort um sie herum von den seltsamen
Wesen aus dem Traum ihrer kleinen Schwester belebt.

65.1 The long grass rustled at her feet as the White Rabbit hurried by — the frightened Mouse splashed his way through the neighbouring pool — she could hear the rattle of the teacups as the March Hare and his friends shared their never-ending meal, and the shrill voice of the Queen ordering off her unfortunate guests to execution — once more the pig-baby was sneezing on the Duchess's knee, while plates and dishes crashed around it — once more the shriek of the Gryphon, the squeaking of the Lizard's slate-pencil, and the choking of the suppressed guinea-pigs, filled the air, mixed up with the distant sobs of the miserable Mock Turtle.

Das lange Gras raschelte zu ihren Füßen, als das weiße Kaninchen vorbeihastete - die ängstliche Maus plätscherte durch den benachbarten Teich - sie hörte das Klappern der Teetassen, als der Märzhase und seine Freunde ihr nicht enden wollendes Mahl teilten, und die schrille Stimme der Königin, die ihre unglücklichen Gäste zur Hinrichtung befahl - wieder nieste das Schweinebaby auf dem Knie der Herzogin, Noch einmal erfüllte der Schrei des Greifen, das Quietschen des Schieferstiftes der Eidechse und das Würgen der unterdrückten Meerschweinchen die Luft, vermischt mit dem entfernten Schluchzen der unglücklichen Spottschildkröte.

So she sat on, with closed eyes, and half believed 66.1
herself in Wonderland, though she knew she had
but to open them again, and all would change to
dull reality — the grass would be only rustling in
the wind, and the pool rippling to the waving of the
reeds — the rattling teacups would change to tinkling
sheep-bells, and the Queen's shrill cries to the voice
of the shepherd boy — and the sneeze of the baby,
the shriek of the Gryphon, and all the other queer
noises, would change (she knew) to the confused
clamour of the busy farm-yard — while the lowing of
the cattle in the distance would take the place of the
Mock Turtle's heavy sobs.

So saß sie mit geschlossenen Augen da und glaubte sich
halb im Wunderland, obwohl sie wußte, daß sie sie nur
wieder zu öffnen brauchte, und alles würde sich in dumpfe
Wirklichkeit verwandeln - das Gras würde nur noch im
Wind rascheln, und das Plätschern des Teiches würde sich
in das Wogen des Schilfs verwandeln - das Klappern der
Teetassen würde sich in das Bimmeln der Schafsglocken
verwandeln, und die schrillen Schreie der Königin würden
sich in die Stimme des Hirtenjungen verwandeln, und
das Niesen des Babys, der Schrei des Greifen und all die
anderen seltsamen Geräusche würden sich (das wusste sie)
in das wirre Geschrei des geschäftigen Hofes verwandeln,
während das Wiehern des Viehs in der Ferne den Platz des
schweren Schluchzens der Spottschildkröte einnehmen
würde.

67.1 Lastly, she pictured to herself how this same little sister of hers would, in the after-time, be herself a grown woman; and how she would keep, through all her riper years, the simple and loving heart of her childhood: and how she would gather about her other little children, and make their eyes bright and eager with many a strange tale, perhaps even with the dream of Wonderland of long ago: and how she would feel with all their simple sorrows, and find a pleasure in all their simple joys, remembering her own child-life, and the happy summer days.

Und schließlich stellte sie sich vor, wie diese ihre kleine Schwester später einmal selbst eine erwachsene Frau sein würde, und wie sie sich in all ihren reiferen Jahren das einfache und liebevolle Herz ihrer Kindheit bewahren würde, und wie sie ihre anderen kleinen Kinder um sich scharen und ihre Augen mit manch seltsamer Geschichte zum Leuchten bringen würde, vielleicht sogar mit dem Traum vom Wunderland aus längst vergangenen Zeiten, und wie sie mit all ihren einfachen Sorgen mitfühlen und sich an all ihren einfachen Freuden erfreuen würde, indem sie sich an ihr eigenes Kinderleben und die glücklichen Sommertage erinnerte.

68.1 **THE END**
DAS ENDE

Möwenstein Books

www.mowenstein.com

Renowned Authors

H. G. Wells · Ernest Hemingway
H. P. Lovecraft · Lewis Carroll
Franz Kafka · Friedrich Nietzsche
Albert Einstein · Oscar Wilde
Hans Christian Andersen

Notable Works

Frankenstein · *Alice in Wonderland*
Heart of Darkness · *The Great Gatsby*
Siddhartha · *The Metamorphosis*
Thus Spoke Zarathustra

Translation Services

We offer translation services in various languages, including German, Spanish, Chinese, Korean, Arabic, and more. For custom translations or revisions, please contact us at:

Email: translation@mowenstein.com

Our Collections

Franz Kafka Collection

- The Metamorphosis / Die Verwandlung
- The Trial / Der Prozess
- The Castle / Das Schloss
- and many more...

Pakt mit dem Teufel

- Faust Parts I & II by Johann Wolfgang von Goethe
- Doctor Faustus by Christopher Marlowe

Portraits of Irishmen

- The Picture of Dorian Gray by Oscar Wilde
- A Portrait of the Artist as a Young Man by James Joyce

Children's Classics

- Winnie-the-Pooh / Pu der Bär
- Brothers Grimm Fairy Tales
- Fairy Tales Told for Children
    - Author: Hans Christian Andersen

Visit Us

At Möwenstein Books, we are committed to providing high-quality bilingual editions of classic works. Explore our collections and discover more titles across various genres and languages.

Website: www.mowenstein.com